The
Book
of
Risks

The Book of Risks

Fascinating Facts About the Chances We Take Every Day

LARRY LAUDAN

John Wiley & Sons, Inc.

New York • Chichester • Brisbane • Toronto • Singapore

Composition: Impressions, a division of Edwards Brothers, Inc.
Design: Tenenbaum Design

This text is printed on acid-free paper.

Library of Congress Cataloging-in-Publication Data
Laudan, Larry
    The book of risks: fascinating facts about chances we take every day /
Larry Laudan
        p.   cm.
    Includes index.
    ISBN 0-471-31034-4 (paper)
    1. Risk perception—United States—Statistics. 2. Risk
assessment—United States—Statistics. I. Title.
HM256.L38   1994
302'.12—dc20   94-6762

Printed in the United States of America.
10 9 8 7 6 5 4 3 2 1

*For all those who think that knowing
is better than not knowing.*

Contents

Thinking about Risks

No other society in history has been as sensitized to risks, dangers, and threats to life and limb as our own. If the food we eat isn't killing us, then it is the air we breathe, or the water we drink. Our fellow human beings are overpopulating the planet, stretching its limited resources beyond the breaking point. Our children return from school fretting about greenhouse gases, the ozone layer, and nuclear winter—the latter produced either by our own stupidity or by a fiery encounter with a comet or asteroid. Parents worry about whether to let Johnny have that peanut butter sandwich because they read somewhere that peanuts carry a potential carcinogen, aflatoxin. We have been told to avoid meat, milk, cigarettes, alcohol, fats, small cars, breast implants, sunny beaches, tap water, smoke-filled rooms, high-rise hotels, nonorganically produced vegetables, and terrorist-infested foreign countries—to mention only a few.

If anyone bothered to keep a list of the risks we are routinely warned about—and doubtless some of us *do* keep such lists—it would fill multiple volumes. More to the point, if we *acted* on all this advice, life would become very dull indeed. In fact, because virtually everything is risky to some degree or other, we would be reduced to total inactivity. You doubt that everything is risky? Ponder this: Hundreds of thousands of Americans are injured each year on their beds, and tens of thousands are done harm by their toilet bowl cleansers or by the change they carry in their pockets. Annually, tens of thousands of Americans inadvertently set their clothing on fire. Another hundred thousand or so are injured by their clothing seriously enough to require emergency medical treatment.

The idea of curtailing everything risky begins to unravel in the face of such facts. We can't give up our beds, our clothes, our toilets, and our currency all in the name of risk management. Because risks lurk everywhere, our risk-aversive behavior is sometimes comic, sometimes absurd—that is, if we can briefly distance ourselves from our situation. As perils go in and out of fashion, we find ourselves doing today exactly what we were urged to avoid yesterday. We are warned, "Avoid aspirin because it causes stomach ulcers" at the same time that we are admonished, "Take aspirin to avoid the risk of strokes." "Alcohol is dangerous to your health." But, of course, "Red wine reduces the chances of a heart attack." "Buy fire-retardant pajamas for your children"; however, as the fine print warns us, "Fire-retardant materials may be carcinogenic."

As we adjust and readjust our actions to keep up with the latest pronouncements of media risk gurus, we resemble nothing so much as drunks staggering from pillar to post with no clear sense of direction. If the stakes weren't so high, our lungings and lurchings would be laughable.

Consider a different sort of example. In the wake of the oil crisis of the mid-1970s, energy conservation measures, designed to reduce the risk of our dependence on foreign oil, became popular. Among those measures were new standards for ventilation and insulation. Yuppies everywhere went out and retrofitted their houses with airtight windows and doors and wood stoves. It later turned out that the added insulation vastly increased the concentration of toxic gases (especially radon) in private homes, while the wood stoves pumped untold quantities of carcinogen-bearing gases into everyone's (now airtight) parlors. We are learning that the world is increasingly like that. Averting or minimizing one risk brings exposure to new ones.

This is a book about many of the risks we face. I try to report the straight facts about them. But I also try to keep it all in perspective by noting some of the contradictions and confusion we get into when we take to heart the numerous bits of information with which we are daily bombarded. This introduction is discusive and didactic; it establishes a context for thinking about risks. The main body of the text is like a "Book of Lists"; it catalogs much of what we know about risks and how to avoid them. If you are already familiar with the basic issues of risk assessment and risk management, you should skip ahead to Chapter 1 without delay.

To the old cliché that a picture is worth a thousand words, our century has added a new twist: A number is sometimes worth a thousand pictures. Let's ponder a few examples. For all the wrenching emotions produced by photographs of stacked corpses and the ovens at Auschwitz or Buchenwald, nothing more nearly conveys the magnitude of the horror than the realization that more than 15 million Jews, Gypsies, homosexuals, and leftists were butchered in the camps. Similarly, no photograph of a hospital deathbed can come as close to summoning up the dread of the 1919 flu epidemic as the realization that it killed more than 20 million men, women, and children. Sometimes the numbers that carry such force are not simple head counts but ratios or percentages. For instance, the fact that four out of every five of the millions of Soviet troops who fought World War II never returned home speaks volumes about how that war took its toll on every family in that country. (Joseph Stalin, with characteristic moral myopia, claimed, "The death of a single Russian soldier is a tragedy, but a million deaths is just a statistic.") The fact that diseases brought from the Old World wiped out more than 80 percent of the millions of Indians living in the New World within two generations is another example of how vividly percentages can convey both information and emotion.

Thus, this is a book about numbers and ratios, for that is the language in which risks to life and limb are most vividly expressed. On the whole, I have deliberately kept my editorializing to a minimum, because the numbers so often speak eloquently for themselves. The book is an experiment of sorts, an attempt to see whether quantities—in this age of numbers and data—still retain the power to inform the mind, to animate the imagination, to guide action, and sometimes to amuse.

I can guarantee, at a minimum, that many of the numbers here will surprise you, for they show vividly that many of the risks of life are quite different from what we might expect.

Risks and You

At some time or other, all of us have played the part of a hypochondriac, imagining that we have some dreaded disease on the strength of the flimsiest of symptoms. Some people have scarcely to hear about a new disease before they begin checking and probing themselves to see if they may be suffering from it. But fear of disease is not our only fear, and neither is risk of disease the only risk we run. Modern life is replete with all manner of threats—to our lives, our peace of mind, our pocketbooks, our families, and our futures. And from these threats come questions that we must pose to ourselves: Is the food I buy safe? Are toys for my children likely to maim them? How risky is that toxic waste dump over in the next county or the nuclear reactor 200 miles upwind from my house? Should my family avoid smoked meats? Am I likely to be robbed on vacation? Should I use a condom? Our uncertainties multiply indefinitely.

Anxiety about the risks of life is a bit like hypochondria; in both, the fear or anxiety feeds on *partial* information. But one sharp difference exists between the two. The hypochondriac can usually turn to a physician to get a definitive clarification of the situation—either you have the suspected disease or you don't. It is much more difficult when anxiety about other forms of risk is concerned, because with many risks, the situation is not as cut and dried.

Risks are almost always a matter of *probabilities* rather than certainties. You may ask, "Should I wear seat belts?" If you're going to have a head-on collision, of course. But what if, heaven forbid, you get hit from the side and end up trapped inside the vehicle, unable to extricate yourself because of a mangled seat belt mechanism? So does this mean that you should lay out the extra cash for an air bag? Again, in head-on collisions, it may well save your life (although, as we will see in Chapter 6, it does less to save your life than a seat belt will). But what if the bag accidentally inflates while you are driving down the highway, thus causing an accident that would never have occurred otherwise?

According to Murphy's famous law, if something can go wrong, it will. Fortunately, Murphy's law is patently false. If even most of the things that could go wrong routinely did go wrong, then none of us would now be around to muse about it. That said, we have to acknowledge that at any time, a dizzying number of things *could* start going wrong. Whether they will, and which ones, all depends on the relevant probabilities.

All of this is another way of saying that nothing we do is completely safe. There are risks, often potentially serious ones, associated with every hobby we have, every job we take, every bite we eat—in sum, with every action. But the fact that there are risks associated with everything we contemplate doing does not, or should not, reduce us to trembling neurotics. Some actions are riskier than others. The point is to inform ourselves about the relevant risks and then act accordingly.

For example, large cars, as everyone knows, are generally safer than small ones in collisions. But how much safer? The answer is that you are roughly twice as likely to die in a serious crash in a small car than in a large one. Yet large cars generally cost more than small ones (and also use more fuel, thus increasing the environmental risks!), so how do we decide when the diminished risks are worth the added costs? The ultimate risk avoider might, for instance, buy a tank or an armored car, thus minimizing the risk of death or injury in a collision. But is the added cost and inconvenience worth the difference in price, even supposing you could afford it?

We cannot begin to answer such questions until we have a feel for the magnitude of the risks in question. So how do we measure the magnitude of a risk? Some people seem to think that the answer is a simple number. We know, for instance, that about 25,000 people per year die in automobile accidents. By contrast, only about 300 die per year in mine accidents and disasters. Does that mean that riding in a car is much riskier than mining? Not necessarily. The fact is that some 200 million Americans regularly ride in automobiles in the United States every year; perhaps 700,000 are involved in mining. The relevant figure that we need to assess a risk is a ratio or fraction. The numerator of the fraction tells us how many people were killed or harmed as the result of a given activity over a certain period of time; the denominator tells us how many people engaged in that activity during that time. *All risk magnitudes are thus ratios or fractions, with values between 0 (no risk) and 1 (totally risky).*

By reducing all risks to ratios of this sort, we can begin to compare different sorts of risks—like mining versus riding in a car. The larger this ratio, that is, the closer it is to 1, the riskier the activity in question. In the case just discussed, we would find the relative safety of car travel and coal mining by dividing the numbers of lives lost in each by the number of people participating in each. Here, it is clear that the riskiness of auto travel is about 1 death per 10,000 passengers; with mining, the risk level is about 4 deaths per 10,000 miners. So although far more people are killed in car accidents than in mining, the latter turns out to be four times riskier than the former. Throughout this book, we will be looking at such ratios. They enable us to compare the risks of activities or situations as different as apples and oranges. If you are risk averse, you will want to choose your activities by focusing on the small-ratio exposures. If your attitude is more devil-may-care, then you are not likely to be intimidated by higher ratios unless they get uncomfortably large, when any but the absolutely foolhardy will make discretion the better part of valor.

Consider, for instance, the figures in the table on the following page. They enable us to take a variety of different risks and reduce them to a common denominator. We see, for example, that hour for hour, skiing is 300 to 400 percent more likely to kill you than flying on a scheduled airline. Three strenuous days of rock climbing exposes a person to about the same risk of death as that run by the average 65-year-old man who goes about his normal business for a fortnight.

ACTIVITIES PRODUCING A 1-IN-1,000 RISK OF DEATH

Activity	Time or Effort Involved
Rock climbing	25 hours
Skiing	340 hours
Working on a farm or in a mine	2.2 years
Being a 65-year-old man	336 hours (2 weeks)
Driving a car	2,000 hours (100,000 miles)
Driving a motorcycle	55 hours (cross-country, one way)
Flying on a scheduled airline	1,200 hours
Regular skydiving	50 hours

Once we understand that risk can never be totally eliminated from any situation and that, therefore, nothing is completely safe, we will then see that the issue is not one of avoiding risks altogether but rather one of managing risks in a sensible way. Risk management requires two things: a modicum of common sense *and* information about the character and magnitude of the risks we may be running. The purpose of this book is to provide a heavy dose of the second. You will find information about a huge spectrum of risks to life and limb. My hope is that it will provide you with the information you need to make reasonable decisions about everything from your choice of life-style to the food you eat and the sorts of gadgets you fill your household with.

I suspect you will discover that the true character of many risks is quite different from what you may have imagined. Too often, we end up preparing ourselves for the improbable risk while failing to take precautions against more likely ones. The media, in particular, have a habit of selecting two or three risks every season to publicize while playing down others. It is not so much that they dishonestly state the dangers associated with the "in" risk as that they fail to set that risk into context. Several years back, for instance, it was fashionable to focus on the risks of the birth-control pill (for example, thrombosis). Those risks were solemnly discussed by talk-show gurus and many women, understandably, became frightened. Sadly, almost no one bothered to point out that *every* pregnancy is roughly 300 percent more life-threatening to a (non-smoking) woman than is a decade on the pill.

Ordinary folk need to know not only what is risky but also what *the level of risk* involved amounts to. Newspaper headlines routinely scream about a cancer risk associated with this or a toxic danger associated with that. Rarely, however, do we learn the magnitude of the risk. If, for instance, the chance of getting botulism from a contaminated can of salmon is only 1 in 10 million, most of us probably would not hesitate to order that salmon salad sandwich. After all, that is much less than the risk of getting hit by lightning. If, on the other hand, the risk is 1 in 100, none of us would knowingly keep a can of salmon in the pantry. But in either case, headline writers are likely to cover the story in the same way:

CONTAMINATED SALMON HITS SHELVES OF LOCAL MARKETS

Such an indiscriminate attitude towards the level of risk doubtless sells newspapers; because virtually everything is risky, there is a limitless set of scare stories that can be cranked out on demand. But this should not be your attitude, because ignoring the level of risk makes sensible risk management impossible. Indeed, my general rule is this: *Unless someone can tell you what level of risk is associated with a given activity, then they have no business telling you that it is risky to begin with.* Always look for the ratios; without them, risks are unintelligible.

"But," you may say, "even if I know how risky something is, I'm still not sure whether I should do it or avoid it. What advice can you give?" This is a tough one, chiefly because it depends on something that only you know: your own tolerance for risk. There is no right answer to the question, "How much risk should I be willing to run?" Or rather, there is no universal answer. You alone can figure out the correct answer in light of your own priorities, values, and attitude towards life. I *can* give you three stereotypes that I often work with when trying to think through these problems for myself. You might try to locate yourself along this spectrum of attitudes to risk; once you have, the rest of the book will then fall naturally into place.

A Profile of Attitudes on Risk: Where Do You Stand?

I can generally class the people I know on a scale of 1 to 3:

1. The High-Stakes Player. This is the person who takes a devil-may-care attitude towards risks, generally supposing that the pleasures derived from an activity invariably outweigh any dangers. He approaches casual sex without a condom, rides a motorcycle without a helmet, reckons that squirreling away money for a rainy day or retirement is a fool's game, smokes and drinks with abandon, and regards the rest of us as overcautious cowards. The only risky actions he refuses are those lacking a challenge or a thrill. Hobbies include skydiving, rock climbing, spelunking, stunt flying, and frequenting singles bars. Alternates holidays between Las Vegas and Atlantic City. Has a job extinguishing fires on oil rigs. Subscribes to *Soldier of Fortune*. Drives a 1965 Mustang and a Harley.

2. The Modest Risk Taker. This person realizes that there are trade-offs in life and is sometimes willing to take on a greater degree of risk than necessary, provided that the payoffs are sufficiently enticing. Unlike the high-stakes player, however, she does not ignore the odds. If the risks outweigh the potential gains, she backs off from the situation, living to play another day. Hobbies include downhill skiing, touch football, and playing the stock market. She's a modest drinker and practices safe sex. Once drove a VW Bus down the Pan-American highway but doubts she would do it again. Works as vice-president of a small manufacturing firm. Sporadically supports the Sierra Club. Subscribes to *The Wall Street Journal*. Drives a new Mercury Cougar.

3. The Risk Minimizer. This person attaches a very high value to preserving her life, fortune, and current status. She avoids even modest risks to what she holds dear. She invests her money exclusively in government-backed CDs, eats only what her doctor recommends, never vacations in Mexico, and is probably overinsured. Her hobbies include chess, stamp collecting, and cross-country skiing. Doesn't drink or smoke; has a reverse osmosis and ultraviolet filtration system attached to her water taps. Joined AARP at 35. Bought a vibrator when the AIDS epidemic started. Works as a tenured associate professor of English at a small state university. Subscribes to *Holistic Nutrition*. Frets about the loss to the gene pool if the spotted owl goes extinct. Drives a 1983 Volvo station wagon.

If you fit profile 1, you probably wasted your money buying this book, because nothing you read here is likely to change your habits in the least. But if you see yourself caricatured in either 2 or 3, there should be much grist for your mill in these pages. The Risk Minimizer will come away from this book with a long laundry list of new activities to avoid. The Modest Risk Taker, by contrast, will probably come away generally reassured. Life, it turns out, is not nearly as risky as the media might lead you to expect; on the other hand, I wager that your assessment of the merits and drawbacks of particular risks may change drastically, because most risks prove not to be quite what they seemed.

If you still find it hard to locate yourself on the scale from risk prone to risk averse, you might want to turn briefly to Chapter 8, which gives a scale of some of the risks we face in ordinary life. By looking through that chapter and identifying the voluntary activities you feel comfortable about engaging in, you'll find out the magnitude of the risks you run in your current lifestyle. Most of us, for instance, don't think twice about taking a walk, even though there is a 1-in-40,000 chance we will be killed as a pedestrian this year. Riding a bicycle is less risky, where we run about a 1-in-130,000 chance of being killed. Events like bathing or flying carry even more negligible risks. A sensible approach to this book would be to place yourself with respect to most of the risks you routinely run and then try to find out whether some one thing or other that you do might not have a risk of injury or death way out of line with the rest. If so, you would be well advised to ponder whether the risks of that activity don't outweigh its benefits.

Most of us find that as risks get more remote than about 1 chance in 10,000, they become difficult to visualize. Here is a very rough rule of thumb for turning such ratios into more intelligible units: An annual risk of death of 1 in a million amounts to the equivalent risk of dying in a car crash if you travel in your car only 1 mile a week for a year; an annual risk of death of 1 in 100,000 poses the same risk as driving your car about 10 miles per week; an annual risk of death of 1 in 10,000 is about the same as what you run if you drive your car about 100 miles a week. Of course, estimates of the risk of a car crash depend on your age, the size of your car, the kind of driving you do, and numerous other factors. But this rule of thumb offers a fairly good base of comparison for risks in the range of 1 in a million to 1 in 10,000. Another easy-to-understand baseline is this: A risk of 1 in 100,000 is the risk that the average 65-year-old woman runs that she will die *within the next hour.* In short, such risks are really very small indeed.

I have gone out of my way in the chapters that follow to state the facts in as nonhysterical a fashion as I can. For almost every risk that is described, I indicate our current knowledge about the level of the risk in question. Even so, I must emphasize that this book does *not* pretend to tell you what risks you should run or what choices you should make. What it does aim to do is to give you the information to make decisions, in light of your own tolerance for, or aversion to, risks and the pleasures that risky activities can bring. Beyond that, many of the risk figures here are interesting in themselves, not least because they underscore some of the comic dimensions of our risk behavior.

Misconceptions About Risk

Numerous academic studies show that there is a large gap between the average person's guess about the magnitude of given risk and its true threat. This would scarcely be surprising if we were dealing only with very exotic or rare events. But the fact is that even with respect to routine risks that we all run (for example, heart attack, cancer, or traffic fatality), there is generally a huge discrepancy between the true magnitude of a risk and the layperson's perception of it. For instance, questionnaire research shows that most people suppose that the chances of their dying of a heart attack to be about 1 in 20; in fact, the risk is closer to 1 in 3. Similarly, the average American reckons the odds of his or her dying in a car accident this year to be about 1 in 70,000; the real figure is closer to 1 in 7,000.

But although we chronically tend to minimize or underestimate the size of common risks, there is also a reverse tendency to exaggerate the size of rare or unusual ones. For example, many Americans regard botulism poisoning or death by tornado as several thousand times more common than they actually are. Risk analysts have theories to explain these divergences between perceived risks and real ones. Usually, they argue that the risks that receive much media attention (like botulism or severe tornadoes) eventually come to be perceived as commonly occurring events, whereas routine causes of death and injury (like heart attacks) are considered so unnewsworthy that people usually learn about them only when they occur in their immediate family or circle of friends.

Whatever the explanation of these discrepancies, their existence is of more than merely academic interest. Because the things we decide to do depend, in part, on our judgments about how risky they are, it follows that if we misjudge the size of a risk by as much as 1,000 percent—and that is the usual level of error between the normal person's perception of a risk and its true value—then most of us are, most of the time, making badly ill-informed decisions. By underestimating common risks while exaggerating exotic ones, we end up protecting ourselves against the unlikely perils while failing to take precautions against those most likely to do us in.

Risks and Public Policy

Insofar as we have options and choices, each of can narrow the risks to which we *voluntarily* expose ourselves. However, many of the risks to which we are exposed are not ones that we can lessen by individual choice. If, for instance, you work in the chemical industry, you are exposed to certain risks that are beyond your individual power to control. If you live in Los Angeles or Mexico City, there are dangers associated with breathing the air that you have no choice but to accept, short of wearing a gas mask. If you are a pregnant woman, there are certain risks inherently associated with pregnancy and childbirth that are simply unavoidable by any action on your part.

In modern society, many risks that are a part of daily life can be reduced, if at all, only by *collective* action. This is where public policy comes into the picture. Risks from disease, the environment, the work place, and crime—all these and numerous others could be diminished if we were collectively minded to do so. For instance, the risks of crime could be vastly diminished either by increasing the size of our police forces, by eliminating the conditions that breed crime, or by a combination of both. Risks from and to the environment could also be mightily reduced by better public transportation, a higher tax on gasoline, mandatory electric cars, or a variety of other measures.

The point, obviously, is that risk reduction—as desirable as it is in its own right—is not cost free. Every diminution of risk, whether in the home, the workplace, or in the streets, has a price tag attached. Sometimes the price is in dollars; other times, it is in jobs or inconvenience or infringements of our rights to privacy and liberty. We must, as a society, decide what levels of risk we find acceptable or how much we are prepared to pay to reduce risks by specific amounts. If money were no object, many risks could be made vanishingly small. But, of course, money *is* an object. With unlimited resources, we could, for instance, make every smokestack in America benign. We could set higher standards for the quality of food. We could test drugs even more thoroughly than we do already. We could make the workplace, the highways, and the streets much safer. But paying for just these few items would require most of the country's domestic national product.

How, given that resources are in short supply, can we make collective, coherent judgments about how to spend our risk-reduction dollars? And because individual tolerances for risk vary enormously, *whose* level of risk should become the norm? The high-stakes player's? The risk minimizer's? Or someone's in between? There are no easy answers to these questions, but there are at least two general principles that should guide our choices but rarely do.

The first (and obvious) principle is that our collective risk dollars should be used to tackle the most serious risks first and that relatively minor risks (such as asbestos insulation in public buildings) should receive treatment and attention only after the largest risks have been tackled. The second principle is that we should stretch our risk dollars to ensure that the money spent reducing a particular risk is commensurate with the reduction achieved. We could, for example, mandate the installation of two air bags in every vehicle produced in the United States. The cost would be approximately $5 billion per year. It is optimistically estimated that even if seatbelts were universally used, compulsory air bags would save an additional 2,000 or so lives per year. That means we would be paying approximately $2.5 million for every life saved.

By contrast, we could fit every car with a governor that would keep its speed under 70 mph. This would cost about $500 million per year and is estimated to be capable of saving about 1,000 lives per year, for about $500,000 per life saved. Obviously, there is much more bang for the buck with the second option.

Consider a different sort of choice. If you don't wear seat belts, air bags do a great deal to reduce your risk of dying in a head-on crash. But if you are conscientious about wearing a proper seat- and lap-belt, then airbags make only a small additional contribution (3 to 4 percent) to reducing your risk of dying in a crash. Under those circumstances, is it worth the several hundred dollars extra to buy a car fitted with air bags? Some car manufacturers, who originally opposed mandatory airbags, quickly changed their tune on the issue once they realized that they could appeal to your desire to protect yourself and your family and thereby persuade you to fork out the additional cash. But unless you are unusually risk averse, the added cost of air bags is scarcely worth the reduced risk they offer in tandem with seat belts. (Not to mention the remote possibility that sodium azide, the caustic gas that is the usual propellant for filling the air bags in the event of a crash, could be accidentally released.)

Calculations such as these are rarely factored in when governments enact new safety standards or procedures. For instance, the Environmental Protection Agency (EPA) has proposed a number of rules regulating exposure levels to various chemicals. In some cases, these are extremely cost effective. The implementation of certain EPA rules concerning drinking water costs about $200,000 for every life saved. Virtually all of us would regard that as money well spent. On the other hand, some proposed EPA rules on wood preservatives involved a cost of roughly $5,700,000,000,000 for every life saved! Precautions of that sort border on madness.

Sadly, neither the political process in this country nor the myopic focusing mechanisms of the media encourages rational social policies about risk management and reduction. How much we spend on a particular risk depends much more on its visibility in the media, or on its appeal to a well-organized special interest group, than on an objective appraisal of its comparative threat to our lives or our well-being. As you will see over and over again in the following pages, our society frequently invests many resources to reduce what are already minor risks while wholly ignoring relatively inexpensive measures that would allow us to reduce some rather large risks drastically.

Government Double-Speak

We can hardly expect that special interest groups will go out of their way to set their favorite risks in a comparative setting; after all, their principal aim is to hype them, and that normally means *not* drawing comparisons between them and other risky activities. However, we have a right to demand more than this from government officials. Unfortunately, we rarely get it. Consider two recent examples, both involving government refusal to speak clearly to the American people about risk: the case of exposure to passive tobacco smoke and the occurrence of cancer-producing chemicals in foodstuffs.

In January 1993, the EPA announced that it had determined that exposure to secondary, or passive, tobacco smoke was a "dangerous and major health risk." Specifically, the EPA estimated that if you are over 35 and are in environments at work or in other public places where you are exposed to such smoke, the chances of your contracting fatal lung cancer from exposure to that smoke are about 1 in 30,000 each year. Is that a high risk or a low one?

Most of us find it difficult to come to terms with such odds or even to know quite what they mean; many Americans simply internalized the fact that exposure to secondary smoking was dangerous and to be avoided. On the strength of the EPA announcement, city councils across the land rushed to ban smoking in public places; employers, ever nervous about litigation, instituted new (or expanded existing) smoking bans in the workplace. But as we have observed before, everything is dangerous to some degree or other; in cases like this, the essence is in the details. Those details take on flesh and blood if we draw a few comparisons with other routine activities:

Drinking two glasses of milk a day poses a greater threat of death from cancer than a lifetime of exposure to secondary smoking.

If you keep a pet bird at home, you are 500 percent more likely to get lung cancer than you are from exposure to secondary smoke.

Eating a smoked pork chop once a week is twice as likely to kill you as secondary smoke will.

If you are exposed to secondary smoke but eat green spinach once a week, you are *less* likely to die of cancer than if you are never exposed to smoke and eat no spinach.

Driving a small car rather than a large one is much more likely to kill you than a lifetime of exposure to secondary smoke.

Not a single press release from the EPA, the Office of the Surgeon General, or the Centers for Disease Control (all of which rang noisy alarms about this new danger) took the slightest pains to compare the risks of secondary smoke exposure with other risks of ordinary life. One can see why, of course; if most Americans realized how the threat from secondary smoke stacked up against other humdrum risks, they could scarcely be mobilized to take the problem very seriously.

If the passive smoking case illustrates one kind of failure on the part of authorities to set risks in context for the public, a different sort of problem has been created by the Envi-

---

THE GREAT CARCINOGEN SHELL GAME

Many objectionable substances (like asbestos, DDT, tobacco smoke) contain potential cancer-causing carcinogens. Often, our judgment that a substance is carcinogenic depends chiefly upon evidence that it induces cancer in rodents when administered in massive doses. All of the following substances carry possible human carcinogens, i.e., they produce tumors in rodents. Importantly, the carcinogenicity is not due to any additives or pesticide residues; it occurs naturally in the substance or its production:

Bacon	Milk
Booze (alcohol is a carcinogen)	Mushrooms
Bread	Mustard
Broccoli	Parsley
Cabbage	Parsnips
Celery	Peanuts
Coffee	Pepper
Colas	Shrimp
Cooked meats	Strawberries
Figs	Tap water (chloroform from chlorine)
Fruit	Tea (herbal)

ronmental Protection Agency's policy on pesticides and other carcinogens in food. What guides the EPA in these matters is the so-called Delaney Clause, an amendment to the Food Additives Act passed by the U.S. Congress in 1958. That clause requires the EPA to ban any food additive that has been shown to produce cancer in rodents or humans. On paper, the idea sounds entirely reasonable; after all, who wants to get cancer from the food they eat?

In practice, however, the law has produced a series of crazy decisions and actions. One familiar worry about the law is its unproven assumption that substances that cause cancer when administered in massive quantities to rodents will have the same effect on humans given doses that are often *one-millionth* the size. We have enormous evidence that many substances that are cancer-producing in certain mammals are not carcinogenic in others. Even within one species, some substances produce cancers in males but not females, or vice versa. If it is difficult to make reliable inferences about cancer causation between individuals of the same species, those difficulties are magnified a thousandfold when we attempt to draw conclusions among different species. That is, something that causes cancer in rats may not do so in humans; likewise, something that produces no cancers in rats may be highly carcinogenic to humans. This standard of safety is doubly misleading because it produces both false negatives *and* false positives in abundance.

But there is a much more serious problem than this with the EPA's use of the Delaney Clause. What we now know, which nobody suspected back in 1958, is that not all carcinogens are artificial; some are *naturally occurring* substances. Still worse, they occur naturally in most of the plants we eat. For instance, 40 percent of the chemicals in apple juice have been found to be carcinogenic in laboratory studies. (For other examples, see the box on page 20). During the last few years, two prominent cancer researchers at Berkeley studied the chemicals occurring naturally in a cup of coffee and concluded that *one* cup of java contains about the same weight (in milligrams) of carcinogenic material as *all* the pesticide residues that the average American consumes in the course of a year!

The EPA irony is this: When carcinogens are present in nature (as in apple juice, coffee, or any of hundreds of other foodstuffs carrying them), the EPA does nothing whatever either to warn citizens about them or to regulate their presence in the food chain. However, if a food producer adds *any* synthetic chemical to a food product, that additive must be absolutely carcinogen free. Otherwise it is prohibited, *even when its carcinogenicity is much less than that of the food to which it is being added.* This policy poses a harsh dilemma for farmers and others in the food-producing industry. They know perfectly well that even organically produced food contains many potential carcinogens. Yet the EPA prohibits the use of any pesticide with similar, possibly deadly ingredients. Understandably, farmers wonder why a carcinogen that nature put there in abundance is permissible when they are prohibited from using pesticides that leave minuscule residues by comparison. There is no coherent answer to this question except to note—as I do on other occasions in this book—the powerful influence of the myth that what is natural cannot really be risky.

Instead of having a government that explains that small doses of potential carcinogens (whether natural or artificial) are things that we can—and have—managed to live with, we see episodic (and tax-funded) public panics about carcinogenic additives. And we remain uninformed about the natural carcinogens we ingest in much greater abundance all the

time. Consumers need to understand that avoiding carcinogens altogether is not only unnecessary but impossible. The
real issue is one of managing their consumption in a reasonable way.

Once risks like secondary smoke or food additives are
set in context, they often appear less threatening than they
seemed before—and much less threatening than they are
usually represented in the media. Unfortunately, fear-
mongering officials, who get paid to paint the risks of everyday life in highly dramatic fashion, usually fail to set things in
context. They simply announce in funereal tones that "such-
and-such causes cancer" or "doing thus and so produces heart
attacks."

Sadly, these exaggerated reports of the dangers of exposure to secondary smoke or food additives are not isolated
cases. Time and again, government-induced hysteria about
relatively low-level risks has led to silly or premature reac-
tions. A current case in point may be the fuss about the
depletion of the ozone layer and the increased risk for skin
cancer that this will supposedly cause. For years, governments and environmentalists around the globe claimed that
damage to the ozone layer caused by pollutants would produce widespread skin cancer and eye cataracts. (The United
Nations went so far as to predict that a 10 percent depletion
of the ozone layer would cause an additional 300,000 skin
cancers and almost 2 million additional cataracts every year.)

Recent, if inconclusive, evidence suggests to the contrary
that even as the ozone layer shrinks, radiation levels in many
places on the earth's surface are *decreasing* rather than increasing. For instance, although ultraviolet radiation increased
over southern Canada during the early years of this decade,
those same levels significantly decreased over Britain, despite
ozone losses in the skies over both countries. It is at least a

plausible hypothesis that natural fluctuations in radiation reaching the earth's surface are much greater than any such changes thus far induced by industrialization. Moreover, evidence is now emerging from work at Brookhaven National Labs that about 90 percent of the sun's rays responsible for causing the most serious skin cancers (melanomas) fall in a range that the ozone layer does little to block. If these preliminary results hold up, then this means that future decreases in the ozone layer, should they occur, would have only a marginal effect on the rate of melanoma.

As the material in the following chapters will make clear, most risks to life and limb are not what we—aided and abetted by years of media obfuscation—have taken them to be. Many of our fears are largely baseless, just as many of the things we regard as safe turn out to be much more dangerous than we thought.

1

Risks of Accidents

An *accident* in ordinary parlance, is whatever is not on purpose. In the risk business, this term refers more specifically to events that produce *unintended* damage, injury, or death. Following the practice of agencies that collect accident-related data, I will divide accidents into two classes: those related to transport (which account for about half of all accidental deaths) and all others. This second group will be the focus of this chapter; transport accidents will be discussed in Chapter 2.

With few exceptions, accident rates in the United States have fallen drastically over the last two generations. Whether at work or at play, in the home or on the road, Americans are less accident-prone than at any time since record-keeping on the subject began. Despite these precipitous declines, however, accidents rank as the fourth largest cause of death. Their seriousness is greater even than this ranking suggests because accidents strike especially hard at healthy folks from the ages of 15 to 44, unlike many fatal diseases, which chiefly target the elderly. Indeed, accidents are the principal killers of Americans under age 37.

In this chapter, we will look at many common (and some bizarre) sources of accidental injury and death. One caution:

As used here, the term *accident* refers to an event producing either death or injuries sufficiently serious to require immediate medical attention—usually in a hospital emergency room. Much of what we know about accident rates comes from hospital logs. Accidents producing property damage without injury or with injuries too minor to require prompt medical attention are not included.

As the facts presented in this chapter make plain, one of the most persistent and startling facts about accident risks is that men are almost invariably exposed to higher levels of risk than women, whether on the playing field, on the job, or at home.

ACCIDENTAL DEATHS

An American dies from an accident every six minutes.

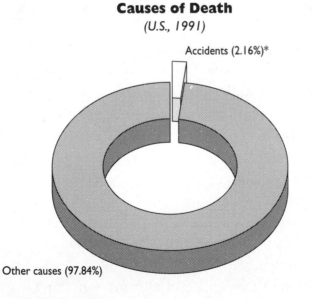

Causes of Death
(U.S., 1991)

Accidents (2.16%)*

Other causes (97.84%)

*Excluding transport

Your odds of dying from some sort of accident this year: 1 in 2,900.

The age group least at risk for a fatal accident: 5–14 years (a 1-in-9,000 chance annually). The age group most at risk: 75+ (a 1-in-700 risk).

The riskiest month for fatal accidents of all sorts: July.

The odds that someone *in your household* (of four) will die from an accident this year: 1 in 750.

In *every* major category of accidental death (including those involving autos, falls, drowning, fires, poisoning, and firearms), men die in higher proportions than women. Either men are more accident-prone or they lead riskier lives, or both.

If you are a divorced man, you are four times more likely to die in an accident than if you are married.

Sites of Fatal Mishaps
(U.S., 1990)

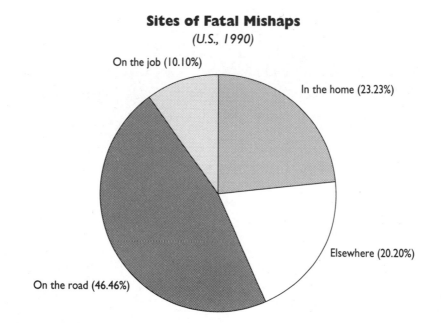

On the job (10.10%)

In the home (23.23%)

Elsewhere (20.20%)

On the road (46.46%)

Some Causes of Accidental Death
(U.S., 1989)

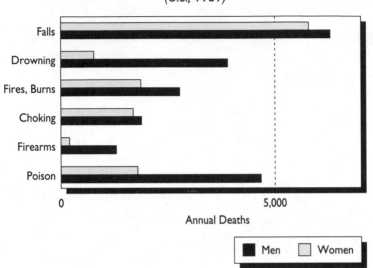

Annual Deaths

Men   Women

If you are a divorced woman, you are more than twice as likely as a married woman to die in an accident.

Accidents kill slightly (about 10%) more men than do strokes.

A man is 250% more likely to die by accident in general (and 500% more likely to die by drowning, in particular) than a woman is.

If you are between 25 and 50, you are far more likely to die from accidental poisoning than from accidents involving drowning, suffocation, or firearms.

The NRA's favorite statistic: National Safety Council figures show that you are 600% more likely to die by accidental poisoning than by a firearms accident. You are also twice as likely to die by accidentally suffocating yourself than from a firearms accident.

General Causes of Accidental Death*
(U.S., 1991)

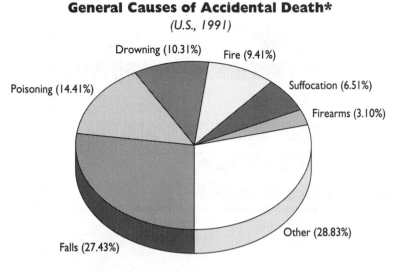

Drowning (10.31%)   Fire (9.41%)

Poisoning (14.41%)   Suffocation (6.51%)

Firearms (3.10%)

Other (28.83%)

Falls (27.43%)

Excluding Transportation

An answer to the restaurateur's prayer: You are more likely to kill yourself accidentally by choking on some *nonfood* stuff than on the food you eat.

This year, you run a 1-in-6,000,000 chance that something will enter some orifice other than your eyes and throat, thereby killing you.

You are 400% more likely to die from falling than from something falling on you.

The young are more likely to die from drowning than from falls. The old are much more likely to do the reverse. Even so, 22% of all drowning deaths occur among those over the age of 75.

The risk of a person dying after a fall from six stories: 90%. The likelihood of a cat dying from such a fall: 10%.

Women who use tampons face a 1-in-100,000 risk of dying this year from toxic shock syndrome.

Risks You Will Die This Year Falling

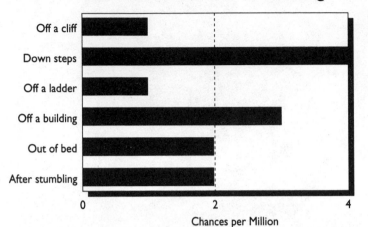

Chances per Million

FREE FALL

The longest nonfatal fall known occurred when an air hostess for a Yugoslavian air-line dropped—without a parachute—33,000 feet over Czechoslovakia and survived.

The risk of death by drowning this year: 1 in 50,000.

The most risky month for drowning: July. Least risky: November.

Don't go near the water! A sizable minority (40%) of deaths by drowning occur to those deliberately swimming or playing in the water. The majority of drowning deaths involve those who ended up in the water by accident (for example, because of a capsized boat, falling off piers, and so on)!

The lifetime risk that you will be killed by a dog: 1 in 700,000. The most likely culprit: a pit bull.

The only venomous animal in the United States whose bite stands more than a 5% chance of killing you if it sinks its fangs into you: the coral snake. Bites from other such demons of outdoor mythology as rattlesnakes, scorpions, water moccasins, black widow spiders, and Gila monsters stand a less than 2% chance of killing an otherwise healthy adult.

A POISON PRIMER

There is a saying among toxicologists that whether something is a poison is "all in the dosage." Here's an example of what they mean. A 150-pound man who consumed these amounts of each of these substances at one time would probably die:

Water: 10 quarts
Sugar: 2.5 pounds
Booze (full ethyl alcohol):
　24 ounces
Table salt: 13 ounces
Aspirin: 3 ounces
Formaldehyde: 0.75 ounce
Pure caffeine: 0.5 ounce
Liquid nicotine: 1 teaspoon
Black widow spider venom,
　parathion: 7 drops
Mustard gas, cobra venom:
　1 drop
Dioxin: less than a tenth of
　a drop

The risk that you will die this year from the joint predations of *all* these creatures: 1 in 21 million.

Black men are 600% more likely to die of hunger than are black women.

Psycho generated nightmares put to rest: The risk of dying this year from an accident in your bathtub (or shower): 1 in a million.

Your annual risk of dying

- By suffocation from something lodged in your throat: 15 in a million

- By electrocution: 3 in a million

- By allergy to prescribed drugs: 1 in a million

The risk that you will be accidentally poisoned this year: 1 in 100. The odds that, if poisoned, you will die: 1 in 440.

DEATH BY FIRE

The risk of dying this year of fire or burns among the general population: 1 in 50,000. Among those 75 and older: 1 in 15,000.

You are four times more likely to die by fire in December than in June or in July.

3% of all work-related deaths are caused by fire.

Men are more likely to kill themselves by accidentally setting their clothes alight than are women.

Almost half a million U.S. residences each year have a fire serious enough to cause structural damage.

The most common cause of household fire: smoldering cigarettes.

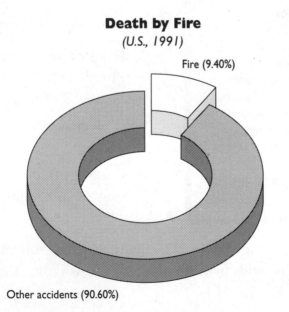

Death by Fire
(U.S., 1991)

Fire (9.40%)

Other accidents (90.60%)

FATAL FIRES

Number of people burned at the stake during the first two decades of the Inquisition: 8,800.

On April 27, 1865, the steamboat *Sultana* caught fire on the Mississippi, killing more than 1,500 people.

The most catastrophic building fire in history occurred during a Chilean evening church service in 1863, killing 2,500. Second-place honors go to a theater fire in Canton, China in May 1845, which resulted in 1,670 casualties.

The worst U.S. fire on land was a forest fire that surrounded Peshtigo, Wisconsin, in October 1871, killing 1,182.

A hot night on the town—worst instances of fire casualties at night spots:

Austrian opera house fire, 1881: 850 dead

Polish circus fire, 1883: 430 dead

Chicago theater fire, 1903: 602 dead

Boston nightclub fire, 1942: 491 dead

Shop 'til you drop: A department store fire in Brussels in 1967 killed 322.

You are 250 times more likely to die of fire than by being blown up.

If you have a fire at home, you are almost 400% more likely to die from the smoke than from the fire. (The proportion of American homes without a smoke detector: 33%.)

Houses without smoke detectors are 600% more likely to be the site of a fatal fire than houses equipped with detectors.

The likelihood that an automatic sprinkler system will fail to operate when needed: 1%.

The risk that an automatic sprinkler, although functioning, will fail to control a fire: 5%–7%.

The risk of an electrical fire in a home with aluminum wiring (widely used in the United States from 1965 to 1973) is 5,500% greater than if all-copper wiring was used.

ACCIDENTAL INJURIES

The odds that you will receive an injury at home this year requiring medical attention: 1 in 13. The odds that you will have a *disabling* accident at home: 1 in 81.

If you live on a farm, you face a 1-in-58 risk this year of a disabling injury.

The two most common types of injuries you are apt to receive in an accident: open wounds and sprains.

On average, accidents and injuries (and insurance to cover such injuries) during your lifetime will cost you about 40% of what you pay in federal income taxes.

A man or boy is 25% more likely to be injured than a woman or girl. The only noteworthy exception: ankle sprains.

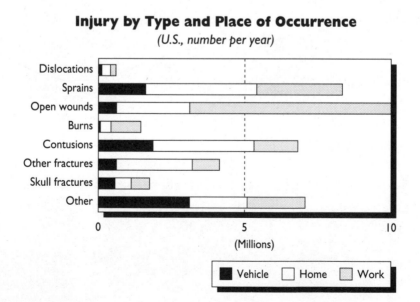

Injury by Type and Place of Occurrence

(U.S., number per year)

The risk you will be injured by a faulty TV this year:
1 in 7,000.

The odds that you will be injured by your toilet bowl
cleanser this year: 1 in 10,000.

Items around the house most likely to produce injuries
requiring medical attention (in *descending* order of threat):

- Stairs and floors
- Chair and beds
- Bicycles
- Doors
- Cutlery

(Are you ready to believe that more than 600,000 Americans each year are injured on chairs and beds? That means
that each of us has a 1-in-400 chance of being injured under
such circumstances.)

In 1989, exactly 28,745 Americans reported injuring themselves with paper money and coins.

The risk that a professional piano player will injure herself
with her instrument: 1 in 2. Principal site of injury: neck.

Have we banned the right stuff? Roughly twice as many
Americans are injured each year by supplies for their pets as
by fireworks. As well, more Americans are injured by their
barbeque grills than by fireworks. Skateboards and sleds
injure ten times as many children as fireworks do. (Nationwide, about five Americans die each year from fireworks
accidents.)

More Americans are injured on metal cans each year than
by the *combined* effects of mopeds, all-terrain vehicles, chain
saws, and minibikes.

A mind-boggler: 40,000 Americans annually admit to being injured by their toilets!

Some 700 to 800 of us each year swallow button batteries.

Another 100,000 are seriously injured by their clothing.

Your risk of injuring yourself seriously enough to require medical attention while shaving this year: 1 in 7,000.

RISKS ON THE JOB

The odds of your dying this year in an accident related to your work: 1 in 11,000.

A typical American worker is 300% more likely to die during leisure time away from the job than at work.

If you work, you are slightly more likely to be *seriously* injured on the job than when you are off work. However,

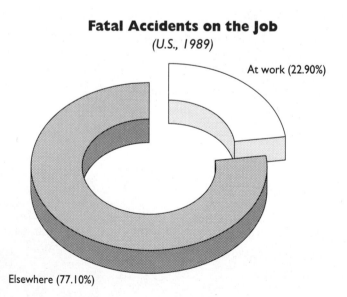

Fatal Accidents on the Job
(U.S., 1989)

At work (22.90%)

Elsewhere (77.10%)

Job Injuries
(U.S., 1991)

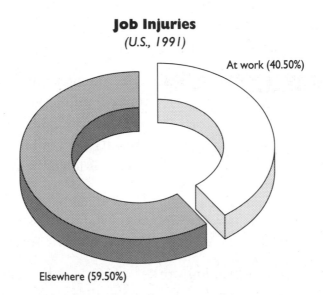

At work (40.50%)

Elsewhere (59.50%)

you are much more likely to receive a *fatal* injury *off the job* than at work.

The body part most likely to be injured at work: the back (22% of all work injuries).

The most common type of disease caused by work: skin disorders.

The odds that you will develop some *chronic* health condition associated with your work: 1 in 250.

The risks of dying this year from a job-related accident or illness if you are

- An airline pilot: 1 in 1,100
- In mining and agriculture: 1 in 2,300
- In transportation: 1 in 4,500
- In government: 1 in 11,000
- In manufacturing: 1 in 23,000

- In sales: 1 in 24,000
- An office worker: 1 in 37,000

Coal mining is the riskiest form of mining as far as dying is concerned. However, its level of job-related *injuries* is lower than most.

For every year that a coal miner works, the risk of eventually dying from black lung disease increases by 1 in 500. (The effects are cumulative.)

All forms of construction work—except painting and paperhanging—are riskier for injuries than coal mining. The riskiest routine construction job is roofing, for which the annual injury risk is 1 in 6.

A steeple jack is 10 times more likely to die on the job than an ordinary construction worker. But height is not always a major risk; a high-wire performer is less likely to die on the job than a routine construction worker.

Many deaths occur every year at construction sites because of unsafe working conditions. New York City has the worst record in the United States, with one construction-related death for every $130 million worth of construction—which

Jobs with a High Risk for Injury

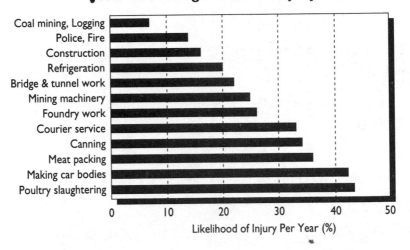

Coal mining, Logging
Police, Fire
Construction
Refrigeration
Bridge & tunnel work
Mining machinery
Foundry work
Courier service
Canning
Meat packing
Making car bodies
Poultry slaughtering

0   10   20   30   40   50

Likelihood of Injury Per Year (%)

works out to be several deaths on average for *every* high-rise construction project.

By contrast, there is one fatality for every $1.1 billion worth of construction in Los Angeles.

Working in the chemical industry involves one of the lowest risk levels for injury. (A grocer is 500% more likely to be injured than a chemical worker.)

The lifetime risk that a current worker in the asbestos industry will contract cancer from a 20-year exposure to asbestos fibers in the workplace: 1 in 500. (Thirty years ago, the lifetime risk was closer to 1 in 5.)

The risk that a meat packer, during a working lifetime, will receive a *permanently disabling* accident at work: 40%.

A curious fact: During 1987 and 1988, those who manufactured clothing for men and boys had almost twice as many accidents on the job as those who made girls' and women's clothes.

The industry with the lowest on-the-job risk of injury: legal services.

The odds that a farm worker's injury was caused by an animal: 17%.

A farm worker is 300% more likely to be poisoned and 250% more likely to have a limb amputated than a nonfarm worker.

It's not just the Post Office department: The third leading cause of death *in the work place* is homicide.

Among women, homicide is the *leading* cause of on-the-job death. This does not mean that more women get killed on the job than men; rather, this tells us something about the low rates of on-the-job deaths of women from other causes, compared to men. More men—and a higher proportion of them—are murdered at work than women. Specifically, 9 out of 10 violent deaths in the workplace claim *men's* lives.

The job carrying the highest risk of being murdered at work: taxi driver.

A LITTLE ACCIDENT GEOGRAPHY

Northern exposure: An Alaskan is 250% more likely to die by accident than someone from Hawaii. Among Canadians, a resident of the Yukon is 310% more likely to die by accident than someone from Ontario.

A French citizen is 50% more likely than an American or Canadian citizen to die by accident.

An American is twice as likely to die accidentally as a Japanese or British citizen.

If you live in Saginaw, Michigan, you are 15 times more likely to die by accident than if you live in Bethlehem, Pennsylvania.

You are twice as likely to die from fire in North Carolina as in Florida.

Oklahomans are 3 times more likely to have serious accidents at home than people in Maine.

Someone who works in shipping on the Great Lakes is 300% more likely to be injured on the job than if he has a comparable job on the high seas.

SPORTS ACCIDENTS

The proportion of professional boxers who suffer brain damage: 87%.

ACCIDENT CALENDAR

Type	Riskiest Month	Safest Month	Difference %
Falls	December	June	22
Drownings	July	November	460
Fires	December	July	320
Poisonings	December	October	13
Firearms	November	March	61
Motor vehicles	July	February	41
Violent crime	August	February	40
Suicide	March	December	21

Sports Injuries and Deaths
(U.S., 1991)

Injuries

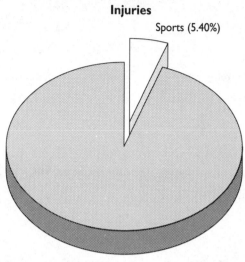

Sports (5.40%)

Other accidents* (94.60%)

Deaths

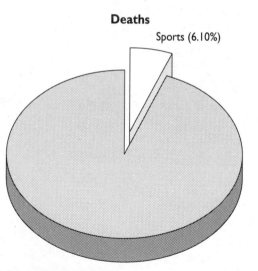

Sports (6.10%)

Other accidents* (93.90%)

*Excluding motor vehicles

Risks of Sports-Related Injury

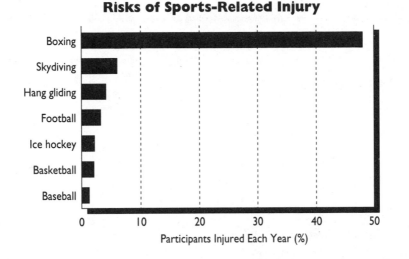

Participants Injured Each Year (%)

An odd bit of sports trivia: In 1991, 5,744 people injured themselves playing billiards. It would probably be indiscreet to inquire too closely into the most common sort of injury pool players sustain.

The annual risk of injury if you play squash regularly: 45%.

French research indicates that the risk of death from down-hill skiing is 1.3 deaths per million *hours* spent on the slopes.

The risk of a fatal accident while rock climbing is 40 deaths per million *hours* spent on the rock face. If we discount the effect of practice, this means that someone who climbs an average of 8 hours per week for 20 years runs close to a 1-in-3 chance of a fatal fall.

Shooting oneself in the foot department: The odds that a hunter's gunshot wounds are *self-inflicted*: 30%. (Roughly 140 hunters die each year in hunting accidents; about ten times that number are injured. The weapon causing the bulk of injuries: the shotgun.)

HISTORY IN A BOX

THE RISK OF SPECTATOR SPORTS

Event	Spectator Deaths
Le Mans car rally crash, 1955	82
Indiana ice show fire, 1963	65
Peruvian soccer riot, 1966	248
British soccer fire, 1985	53
German air show crash, 1988	47
British soccer riot, 1989	93
South African soccer riot, 1991	40

A million Americans are injured each year by their sports equipment.

In 1991, more than 6,000 golfers were injured by their golf carts.

The least risky popular sports: badminton and ping-pong.

2

Travel Risks

Ours is an extraordinarily mobile society. Each year that fictitious creature, the average American, travels more than 9,000 miles by car, flies 1,400 miles, rides a bus almost 500 miles, takes a train for 52 miles, and rides a motorcycle 35 miles. She also walks about 75 miles. In fact, she probably spends more time in transit than anywhere else except in bed or at work. She puts life and limb at risk each time she goes from point A to point B. Motor vehicle accidents alone kill more Americans than diabetes, suicide, homicide, or AIDS. (Since the introduction of the automobile, almost 3 million Americans—equivalent to a city the size of Chicago—have died in auto accidents.) If you are under 45 and male, motor vehicle accidents are more likely to kill you than cancer, heart disease, or any other malady.

Everyone knows that travel carries its dangers, but many misleading myths persist about the relative safety of various forms of getting around. Few people realize, for instance, that it is riskier, mile for mile, to be a pedestrian than to ride a motorcycle. (By a *pedestrian,* I mean a person walking along city sidewalks or country roads and traversing intersections. These figures obviously do not apply to someone walking across a field or hiking along a trail.) Fewer still realize that

Accidental Deaths
(U.S., 1991)

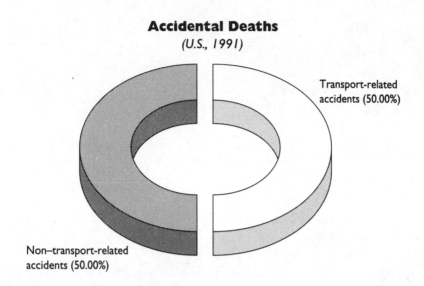

Transport-related
accidents (50.00%)

Non–transport-related
accidents (50.00%)

buses and trains are generally safer than many forms of commercial aviation; so too, under certain circumstances, are private automobiles. How many of us understand that *most* deaths caused by motor vehicle accidents are not the result of collisions between vehicles but of such things as jackknifing or hitting a tree or a pedestrian?

This chapter is about the most common forms of human locomotion and the risks associated with them. If you want to know which are the safest airlines or whether airbags do you any good or how likely you are to survive a crash with a speeding locomotive, read on.

AUTO RISKS

The chance that you will be involved in an automobile accident this year: 8%.

In case you wondered why auto insurance rates vary with age: If you are 19 or under and a licensed driver, your likelihood of having an accident this year is 28%.

Transportation-Related Deaths
(U.S., 1991)

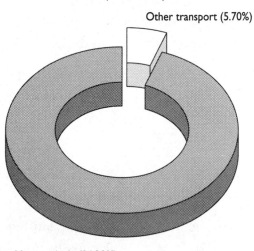

Other transport (5.70%)

Motor vehicle (94.30%)

Your risk of being killed in some sort of motor vehicle accident this year: 1 in 5,800. (This figure includes both pedestrian deaths and deaths involving vehicles other than autos.)

Your risk of dying this year as an occupant of a car: 1 in 11,000.

If you are 19 or under and a licensed driver, your risk of being involved in a fatal accident: 1 in 1,500. Those aged 19 and under constitute about 5%–6% of licensed drivers, but they are involved in more than 12% of fatal accidents.

A driver aged 15–24 is almost twice as likely to be a traffic fatality as an older driver.

About half of all driving fatalities are due to drivers violating traffic rules. The single most frequent offense leading to fatalities: speeding. The second most frequent offense: drunk driving.

A hidden cost of splitting up: If you are a divorced man, you are four times more likely to be a traffic fatality than if you are married. If you are a divorced woman, you are more than twice as likely as a married woman to die on the highways.

Mile for mile, city police are 9 times more likely to have an accident than state police. City police have four accidents every 100,000 miles. The normal driver has a traffic accident roughly every 100,000 miles.

Your risk of being killed in a car accident is about twice as great as your risk of being a homicide victim.

Men drive 65% of the miles driven in the United States. Not surprisingly, therefore, they are involved in far more auto accidents, including fatal ones. If you adjust for the relative number of miles driven, *accident* rates show that women are slightly more accident prone than men (ten versus nine accidents per 1,000,000 miles driven, respectively). Nonetheless, even if a man and woman drive the *same* number of miles per year, the man is more than twice as likely to be involved in a *fatal* accident than is the woman.

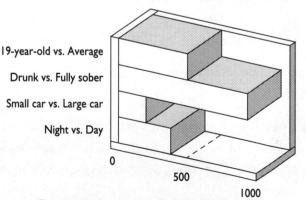

Increased Risk of Fatalities

Percentage of Increase per Each Mile Driven

THE FOLKS IN RED, WHITE, AND BLUE

In 1990, the following types of vehicles were involved in traffic accidents:

Police cars: 22,600
Firetrucks: 5,400
Ambulances: 2,400

This means that 1-in-600 road accidents involved one of these vehicles.

Roughly 45% of all drivers killed in car crashes test positive for blood alcohol.

The risk of having a fatal accident if you are drunk (blood alcohol concentration above 0.15%) and driving is 600%–1,300% greater than if you are fully sober.

You are twice as likely to die on the road if you drive a small car (2,000 pounds or less) than if you drive a large one (4,000 pounds or more).

You can aggregate some of these data this way: Someone driving a small car at night while drunk is about 5,000% more likely to end up as a traffic fatality than someone driving a large car during the day while sober.

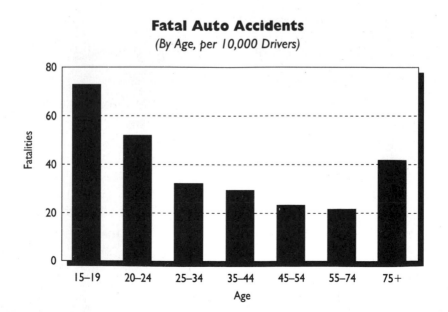

Fatal Auto Accidents
(By Age, per 10,000 Drivers)

A traffic accident occurring on the shoulder of a major highway is 500% more likely to be fatal than an accident on the highway itself.

Trucks are involved in about 25% of all motor vehicle accidents. Nonetheless, truck drivers—especially drivers of tractor-trailer rigs—have a per-mile accident rate that is one-tenth that of the normal driver of a passenger car.

Although heavy trucks make up only about 4% of all registered vehicles, they are involved in 8% of fatal accidents. This is not because they are more prone to accidents, but obviously, if a heavy truck is in an accident, then the prospects for fatalities are much higher. (Moreover, heavy trucks log far more miles and hours on the road per vehicle than passenger cars.)

The proportion of serious rural traffic accidents (for example, on interstate highways) where the ambulance arrives more than half an hour after the crash: 20%.

The chances that your tractor will overturn and kill you this year if you are a farmer: 1 in 25,000.

The risk that a U.S. bridge is obsolete or structurally flawed: 40%.

The risk that a bridge, during its design lifetime, will collapse: 1 in 1,000,000.

The lifetime risk that you will be on a collapsing bridge: 1 in 4,000,000.

Head-on collisions are mercifully rare (3% of all crashes), but they are devastating when they occur because 1 in every 54 produces a fatality.

The risk that a rear-end collision will be fatal: 1 in 2,000.

The convertible owner's nightmare: More than 10% of all traffic deaths arise from cars overturning.

A car that is moving into or out of a parallel-parking slot is 40% less likely to be involved in an accident than one that is angle parking.

The number of motor vehicle accidents you would have to endure to make it likely that you would be killed: 300+.

The added risk of fatalities when interstate rural speed limits went from 55 to 65 mph: 19%. Serious injuries increased by 40%.

The most likely body part to be injured in an automobile accident: the face, which accounts for 21% of all injuries.

Hit the road: You are twice as likely to be injured at work as you are to be injured in your car. Staying home is even worse; you are four times more likely to do yourself an injury at home than in the car. That's the good news for fanatic drivers. The bad news is that you are twice as likely to *die* in your car than because of an accident at work, and you are three times more likely to receive fatal injuries in your car than at home.

Of Americans who work outside the home, 84% travel via private motor vehicle. Because the average person lives 9.2 miles from work, he travels 4,600 miles to and from work annually. So, over a 40-year working lifetime, he runs about a 1-in-500 chance of a fatal accident en route to work.

THE WHERE AND WHEN OF CAR ACCIDENTS

Well over half of all motor vehicle–related deaths occur after dark.

In fact, driving at night is, mile for mile, almost four times more likely to kill you than daylight driving. One reason for the difference is visibility. During the day, a driver's field of vision extends about 1,500 feet in front of the car; at night, headlight beams can illuminate no further than 400 feet.

The proportion of fatal traffic accidents that occur within 25 miles of driver's home: 70%

The Saturday *morning* special: The single riskiest hour of the week for *fatal* traffic accidents is between 2 and 3 A.M. on Saturdays.

The riskiest time for *nonfatal* accidents is Fridays between 4 and 6 P.M.

The safest day for driving: Tuesdays.

The riskiest months for traffic deaths: July and August. The safest months: January and February.

Mile for mile, driving in Alaska, Nevada, Arkansas, or Mississippi is more than twice as likely to kill you as driving in Massachusetts or Connecticut.

Someone driving a car in Turkey is 1,800% more likely to have a fatal accident than someone driving in the United States.

Residents of El Paso or Oklahoma City are 400% more likely to die in traffic deaths than residents of Minneapolis or Indianapolis.

SAFETY DEVICES

The amount by which a lap/shoulder seatbelt reduces fatalities in front-end auto crashes: 42%. The amount by which an airbag on its own does the same: 33%. The *combined* effect of the two: a 46% reduction in front-end fatalities. In other words, the extra $500–$600 laid out for a pair of airbags buys relatively little additional safety (4%) over and above the standard seatbelt restraint. (This fact notwithstanding, Washington has made airbags mandatory in new

---

GEOGRAPHY AND THE COST OF A LIFE

Those who design transportation systems obviously have an obligation to make them safe. But there is never enough money to make them completely safe. How then do we decide which safety features to incorporate and which to forgo? Do we spend our highway safety money on sturdy guardrails, ample lighting, frequent emergency phones along the roadside, reflectors lining the lanes, policemen patrolling every few miles, wide median strips separating lanes of traffic in different directions, or what?

To make such decisions, it is necessary to figure out how many lives each option would be likely to save and how costly each option is. This means deciding how much each life

saved or lost is worth in order to determine whether the cost of the safety feature is reasonable. Transportation departments in different countries have reached very different answers to this question. In the United States, we are generally prepared to lay out $1,000,000 for safety if it will save 0.38 lives. In Portugal, by contrast, that much money is spent on safety only if doing so promises to save 50 lives. The following list shows some other countries' estimations of $1,000,000 worth of human life:

Sweden: 0.81 lives
Belgium: 2.5 lives
Britain: 0.91 lives
France: 2.9 lives
Germany: 1.1 lives
Netherlands: 7.7 lives

cars from the middle of the decade.) Many of us, however, have seatbelts but don't use them. Percentage of Americans who report *never* using a seatbelt: 32%.

It is worth realizing that only about 40% of the fatalities in multiple-vehicle crashes are from front- or rear-end collisions. Fully 30% of fatalities are from side collisions (so-called 3 o'clock and 9 o'clock crashes). Air bags are of little use in averting such fatalities.

Here comes the cost-benefit question again: An energy-absorbing steering column in a passenger car lessens the driver's chances of a fatal injury by less than 1%. To date, studies of cars equipped with antilock brakes fail to show that they do *anything* to reduce the risks or the costs of highway crashes. (We can thus expect that, if Washington is true to type, such brakes will soon be required on all cars.)

Because of the effect of car size on survivability, you are less likely to die in a crash wearing *no* seat belt in a large car than if you are wearing a seat belt in a small car.

Helmets reduce the risks of fatal injuries to motorcyclists by 30% and reduce serious head injuries resulting from bicycle accidents by more than 70%.

BIKES, MOTORBIKES, AND PEDESTRIANS

A motorcyclist is 400%–500% more likely to be in a fatal accident this year than someone riding in a car. Per mile driven, the motorcyclist is about 2,500% more likely to be a fatality than his car-driving counterpart. (The apparent discrepancy arises here because motorcyclists generally drive far fewer miles per year than motorists.)

Deaths on the Road
(U.S., 1991)

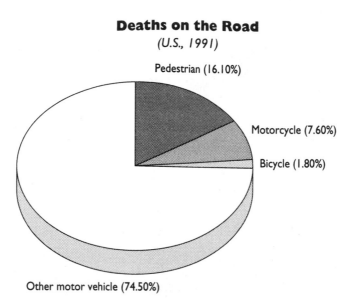

Pedestrian (16.10%)

Motorcycle (7.60%)

Bicycle (1.80%)

Other motor vehicle (74.50%)

The risk that a frequent motorcycle rider will be in a fatal accident this year: 1 in 1,000.

One study found that *three-wheel* motorcycles are involved in an accident approximately every 2,000 miles.

The odds that you will die on your bicycle this year (if you own one): 1 in 130,000.

In 1950, 10% of bicycle fatalities involved persons 25 or over. By 1991, almost 40% of bicycle-related fatalities involved those over 25.

If you ride a bicycle an hour a week for 20 years, your risk of being killed by a motor vehicle: about 1 in 50. In 1990, 32% of bicyclists killed in road accidents had been drinking; almost 23% had blood alcohol levels in the DUI range for motorists.

Strict enforcement of drinking and driving laws in Florida has doubled the number of *drunk bicycle riders* involved in fatal accidents.

Almost one-third of *urban* motor vehicle–related deaths are pedestrians.

The odds that a *pedestrian* killed by a motor vehicle was drunk: 1 in 3.

Running down pedestrians on city streets kills more than half as many people as do *all two-vehicle collisions.*

The odds that a randomly selected pedestrian will be killed by a car this year: 1 in 40,000.

The risk that a pedestrian struck by a car will die:

- In urban settings: 2%
- In rural ones: 5%

Mile for mile, it is far riskier to walk (or jog)—if that activity involves crossing intersections—than to use any motorized transport, including a motorcycle.

Pedestrian deaths are more than double the number of motorcycle-related deaths.

AIR TRAVEL

Worldwide, the chance of your having a fatal accident on your next commercial flight: 1 in 400,000.

Within the United States, the odds of your next trip on a large commercial jet being fatal are 1 in 5,000,000. Your risk of serious injury: 1 in 1,000,000.

On a commuter flight, your risk of death goes up to 1 in 2,600,000. Your risk of serious injury: 1 in 4,000,000.

On a charter flight, the risk of a fatal accident rises to 1 in 160,000.

Transportation-Related Deaths
(U.S., 1991)

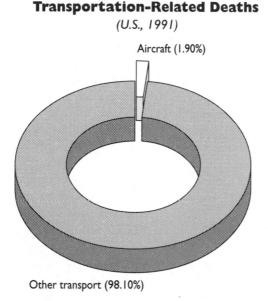

Aircraft (1.90%)

Other transport (98.10%)

Flight-related risks are often expressed in terms of passenger miles. Using that idiom, here are some of your chances of dying in *scheduled* air travel:

- Per mile: 1 in 5,000,000,000.
- If you fly 10,000 miles: close to 1 in 500,000
- If you fly 100,000 miles: close to 1 in 50,000

Mile for mile, *commuter* airlines are about 10 times more likely to have a fatal accident than large airlines. Hour for hour, *private* airplanes are about 100 times more likely to have a fatal crash than large airlines; mile for mile, the figures are even more scary, because private planes generally fly more slowly than commercial jets.

The odds that you will die in an accident on a scheduled airline this year (excluding flight crew): 1 in 350,000.

FLYING VS. DRIVING

The vast majority of airline accidents occur during landing and take-off. This means that the most important question to ask about a proposed flight is not so much how much distance it covers, but *how many stops* it involves. In other words, short and multiple-stop flights are much riskier mile for mile than long, nonstop flights because short hops (say from Boston to New York) involve the same landing and take-off risks as transatlantic flights. Airlines want us to focus on accident rates per passenger mile, because that makes air travel look extraordinarily safe. If you examine accident figures per passenger *flight* rather than per passenger mile, however, a slightly different perspective emerges—as you can see from this hypothetical example:

A safe, low-risk U.S. driver—aged about 40, wearing seat belts, travelling in a heavier than average car on safe roads (like rural interstates)—has a fatality rate of about 1 death per 1.2 billion miles driven. Thus, on a 200-mile trip, the cumulative risk is about 1 in 6 million.

Suppose that same driver were to travel via a large scheduled airliner (noncommuter). His chances of death are then about 1 in 5 million, because that is the ratio of deaths to passenger boardings. Hence, the driver is safer in this case than the flyer. If that seems confusing, simply bear in mind that trips of 200 miles or less are safer by car than by airliner, granted good driving conditions and so on. On longer trips, or with less than excellent drivers, large airlines are safer . . .

. . . Provided, that is, that we are talking about *noncommuter* flights. With commuters, the accident death rate has been about 1 in every 2.6 million passenger boardings. For a commuter flight to be less risky than riding in a car with a safe driver, we would have to be dealing with *nonstop* trips of more than 450 miles. Because the average commuter flight is 125 miles (and few are as much as 450), a sound rule of thumb is that traveling in a large car on good road with an experienced driver is a safer bet than taking a commuter flight—more or less regardless of the distance involved.

Your risk of dying in general (that is, private) aviation:

- Per mile: 1 in 220,000,000
- If you fly 10,000 miles: close to 1 in 22,000
- If you fly 100,000 miles: close to 1 in 2,200

You are three times more likely to have a fatal accident on a small airliner than on a large one.

The risk that a flight you are taking will come dangerously close to having a midair collision with another aircraft: 1 in 40,000.

80% of all air fatalities occur in private aircraft; 6% of those crashes occur because the pilot was high on alcohol or drugs.

A Navy pilot who flies jets for 20 years runs a 23% risk of dying in an aircraft accident. Even so, more Navy test pilots die in car crashes than in plane crashes.

RAREFIED AIR RISKS

Various things that can (but usually don't) go wrong on scheduled flights:

Between 1968 and 1984, almost 700 attempts were made worldwide to hijack airplanes. Roughly half succeeded.

During a seven-year period, 17 pilots of U.S. commercial airlines died in the cockpit (usually of heart attacks); five of these deaths led to fatal accidents that killed a total of almost 150 people.

There are approximately two cabin fires worldwide per year; one of them produces fatalities.

The risk that an aircraft engine will malfunction in flight, requiring shutdown of the engine is between 1 in 50,000 hours and 1 in 14,000 hours (depending on the engine in question). Thus, on a 6-hour flight on a plane with four engines, the probability of a forced engine shutdown is about 1 in 2,000.

Bad weather is the primary cause of about 6% of air crashes.

If a plane encounters severe windshear, the pilot has less than 15 seconds in which to recognize it and take compensatory action.

The risk that someone boarding your next jumbo-jet flight will be caught attempting to bring a gun aboard: 1 in 1,500.

The odds that a piece of luggage loaded on a plane will contain a bomb: 1 in 100,000,000. (The number of bags checked each day in the United States: about 1,000,000.)

In survivable accidents, 47% of the injuries to airline passengers were the result of seats or seatbelts failing to protect passengers as they were designed to do.

On long-haul flights, the risk that some passenger on a jumbo jet will have a medical emergency (often a heart attack) requiring immediate medical attention: 1 in 75.

RISKY AIR SPACE

Some countries are much safer to fly in (or over) than others. Here are the number of fatalities per 1,000,000 flights for various countries between 1973 and 1984:

Turkey: 1,717
Colombia: 510
Netherlands: 384
Belgium: 203
United Kingdom: 57
United States: 37
Germany: 27
Canada: 24
Australia: 1

The extraordinary Turkish figure works out to 1 fatality for every 600 flights.

The figure below underscores the previously mentioned fact that the chief risk factor in flight is not the number of miles flown but rather the number of *stops* made. Because very few accidents occur when a plane is cruising, long, non-stop flights are, mile for mile, very much safer than short flights.

According to a study of airline safety records from the 1980s, these are the airlines with the best safety records in each category:

When Air Accidents Occur: The Phases of Flight

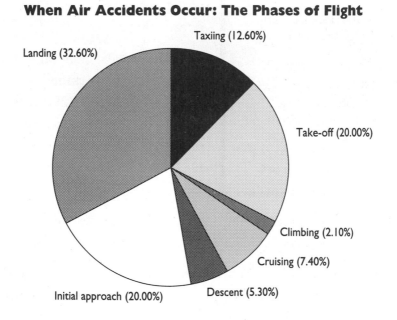

Taxiing (12.60%)
Landing (32.60%)
Take-off (20.00%)
Climbing (2.10%)
Cruising (7.40%)
Descent (5.30%)
Initial approach (20.00%)

- *Large* carriers: American, British Airways, Delta, Lufthansa, SAS, and Southwest
- *Midsize* carriers: All Nipon, America West, Ansett Australia, Canadian Airlines International, and Saudi Arabian
- *Medium-to-small* carriers: Alaska, Finnair, KLM, Malaysian, and Swissair

AIRLINE FATALITY RECORD, 1977–89

(Fatalities per 10,000,000 departures)

Aeroflot: 25

Aloha: 19

Pan Am, JAL: 15

Mexicana, Olympic: 11

Northwest: 5

Continental: 3

US Air, United, Eastern, Air Canada, American: 2

Delta: 1

TWA, Southwest, Canadian, Hawaiian, Alaska, America West, Air New Zealand, Qantas, Lufthansa, British Air, Air France, KLM, Sabena: 0

All enjoyed fewer than 1 accident per 2,500,000 flights.

A large helicopter is 500% more likely to crash (per hour of operation) than a large jet.

The evidence is overwhelming that older pilots (ages 35–60+) have fewer accidents per hour of flying time than younger ones.

Jet aircraft were generally designed for a working life of 20 years. In 1989, 32% of the U.S. airline fleet was 20 years or older. The *average* age of a B707 or a DC-8 in 1990 was 22+ years.

Percent of aircaft accidents attributable, at least in part, to human error: 65%.

The most frequently injured employees in the airline industry: cabin cleaners and cargo handlers. The least frequently injured group: the cockpit crew.

The odds that an aircraft will fall on you and kill you sometime this year: 1 in 25,000,000.

U.S. airports rated the most dangerous by the International Federation of Airline Pilots Associations: Los Angeles International and San Francisco International.

BUSES, TRAINS, AND SHIPS

About 1 in every 1,000 transport-related deaths in the United States during the last decade occurred in the *public* transport sector (which includes passenger buses, planes, trains, and ships).

Intercity buses are handily one of the safest forms of transport for the passenger. Their fatality record is marginally better than trains and substantially better than airplanes. Fatalities by car are about 30–40 times greater per passenger mile than by bus.

Compared to intercity buses, charter buses have half the rate of accidents per mile.

The odds of your dying in an accident on a passenger train

are 1 per 5,000,000,000 passenger miles. Thus, on a trip of 500 miles, your risk of death is about 1 in 10,000,000. Comparable rates apply to scheduled airlines if fatalities on commuter and larger craft are combined.

The percentage of all U.S. railway freight that is classified as "dangerous material": 8%.

The chances that a railroad employee will die in a train accident over a 30-year career: 1 in 250.

In 1991, there were 5,000 collisions between trains and passenger cars, producing 500 deaths. So, as improbable as it seems, your chances of surviving a collision with a train are a tad better than 90%.

The percentage of seamen who claim to have served on a ship that was not seaworthy: 99%.

The odds that a selected merchant ship will sink this year: 1 in 2,000.

The time required to bring a 250,000-ton supertanker to a stop from cruising speed: 21 minutes (during which time it covers three miles).

Collisions between ships account for only 10% of shipping accidents.

3

Health Risks

Opinion polls repeatedly tell us that the only thing Americans worry about more than the environment is their health. This is entirely understandable, for health is clearly preferable to illness. What makes today's preoccupation with health slightly surprising is that Americans are far healthier now than they have ever been. Many diseases that once struck terror into hearts and minds (like smallpox, malaria, plague, pneumonia, polio, TB, and leprosy) have either been completely eliminated or brought under control. Although AIDS is a notable exception, few new mass killers have come along to replace the vanquished ones.

Nonetheless, health—and the various threats to it—remain everyone's abiding concern. After all, more than half of us (57 percent) will die from either heart disease or cancer, if current trends continue. This chapter examines three sorts of health risks: fatal diseases, chronic diseases, and occasional diseases.

One major problem with any comparison of health risks—especially life-threatening ones—is that they differ enormously in their *immediacy*. For instance, AIDS—if you get it—will probably do you in within a few years after onset. Cancer induced by smoking or exposure to radiation, on the other hand, may take 20 to 30 years before its catastrophic effects show up. In making choices about health risks, therefore, it is important to bear in mind the likely time lag between taking a risk and suffering its consequences.

Those with a mind to "live for today" are apt to be indifferent to, and unmoved by, health risks that have a very drawn-out incubation period. Although this is shortsighted, it does make sense to discount long-term risks more than short-term ones. After all, when virtually any of us is confronted with the choice of doing something likely to kill us today versus doing something likely to kill us in two decades, the choice is going to be the lesser of the two evils.

One commonly used measure to grapple with such conundrums is a concept called *years of potential life lost* (YPLL). The idea is that for a 25-year-old, doing something that will kill him in 5 years is much more "costly" than doing something that will kill him in 40 years. Both may involve the same element of risk—the same probability of eventually dying from that activity—but a risk that may extract a clear and present toll is much more costly than one for which the piper needn't be paid for a long time. In the first case, he will have his normal lifespan cut short by some 45 years; in the latter case, the deficit is about 5 years. Thinking about matters in this light inevitably causes a reassessment of many of the threats to health. For instance, heart disease is the single largest killer of Americans, way in front of cancer or strokes. However, heart disease tends to strike the elderly in much greater proportions than their juniors. Cancer, by contrast, kills fewer people but tends to strike somewhat earlier than heart disease. Hence, more YPLLs are lost to cancer than to heart disease—despite the greater incidence of fatal cases of the latter. Specifically, cancers claim about 25 percent more YPLLs than heart disease (if we define the YPLL as a year of life lost before age 65).

The concept of YPLLs has an important, if controversial, bearing on vexing issues in health care economics. It is frequently argued that money devoted to medical research on curing disease should be apportioned on the basis of the number of lives lost to each disease. Thus, some critics of the massive levels of funding devoted to AIDS research claim that—compared to killers such as heart disease and cancer— AIDS receives disproportionately high support. That critique fails to reckon with the fact that AIDS, by virtue of striking people principally in their 20s and 30s, generates far more YPLLs than the bare figure of 20,000 deaths per year, bad as that is, might suggest. Put differently, finding a cure for AIDS would be likely to add about 25–30 years to the life of each potential victim. Finding a cure for heart disease, although it might save far more lives, would probably add only another 5–10 years to the longevity of its average victim.

The two figures that follow vividly illustrate how the assessment of the severity of a risk changes, depending upon whether we simply ask how many lives it claims or how many YPLLs it involves. Some of the differences are quite striking. For instance, accidental deaths appear relatively insignificant compared to cancer and heart disease when we just count the deaths caused. But once we look at the number of lost *years,* accidents loom into first place among the killers of Americans. Just as vividly, homicide, suicide, and AIDS—each of which looks quite insignificant on the first chart—take on quite a different look when we consider them in terms of years lost. What such data drive home is the fact that we need to ask not only how large a risk is but also when it becomes payable. Other things being equal, the sooner a risk extracts its toll, the more that risk is to be avoided.

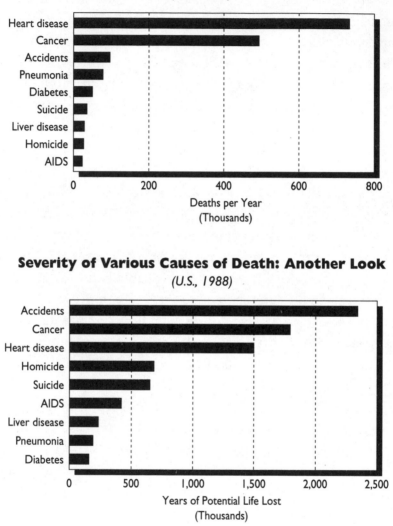

Severity of Various Causes of Death
(U.S., 1988)

Heart disease, Cancer, Accidents, Pneumonia, Diabetes, Suicide, Liver disease, Homicide, AIDS

0   200   400   600   800

Deaths per Year
(Thousands)

Severity of Various Causes of Death: Another Look
(U.S., 1988)

Accidents, Cancer, Heart disease, Homicide, Suicide, AIDS, Liver disease, Pneumonia, Diabetes

0   500   1,000   1,500   2,000   2,500

Years of Potential Life Lost
(Thousands)

INFECTIONS AND EPIDEMICS

At any given moment, each of us has more bacteria in our bodies than living cells. Many of them are harmless, some are essential, and others may lay us low with one disease or other. The wonder is not that we get ill from time to time but that we are ever fully well. Indeed, through most of history, almost everyone spent most of their lives in a state of more or less continuous infection with disease of one sort or another. The worry then was not so much whether you were ill—that was a foregone conclusion—but whether your current ill-ness would kill you. There are, of course, still infections that kill, but most of us now have the relative luxury of being able to worry more about getting sick and less about whether our current disease will prove to be our undoing.

For many of the most common infectious diseases, the risk and frequency of getting them increases as the size of your family increases. For instance, *each* member of a family of five is 50% more likely to have a case of gastroenteritis—and most other highly infectious diseases—than someone from a family of three.

The risk of contracting TB in New York or Washington, D.C., is 2,000% greater than it is in 21 other states.

The risk of dying from a smallpox vaccination: 1 in 100,000. The risk of dying from smallpox during an epidemic, if you are exposed but haven't been vaccinated: 1 in 7.

No Americans died of cholera in 1988.

The risk of contracting the plague in the United States this year: 1 in 25,000,000.

The risk of death if you contract botulism: 70%.

TB now kills fewer than 2,000 Americans per year. Your risk of getting TB is only about 10% what it was in 1950.

HISTORY IN A BOX

EPIDEMICS

In preindustrial Europe, smallpox infected 95% of the population, of which it killed about 14%.

Between 1804 and 1918, New York City had the following epidemics:

- Yellow fever (3 outbreaks): 445 deaths

- Smallpox (12 outbreaks): 7,044 deaths

- Cholera (6 outbreaks): 13,210 deaths

- Typhoid fever (1 outbreak): 200 deaths

- Influenza (1 outbreak): 12,562 deaths

This amounts to a serious epidemic every five years. Other U.S. cities had similar patterns of disease.

Between 1347 and 1351, bubonic plague killed more than 25,000,000 Europeans.

The Great Plague killed 50,000–100,000 Londoners in 1665.

Indigenous Mexicans who died of *European* diseases within two generations of the arrival of the conquistadors: 12,000,000–25,000,000. In Mexico City alone, there were 19 major epidemics in the century after Cortes' arrival.

In 1722, 20,000 Russians died of ergotism (rye bread poisoning).

A cholera epidemic in 1831 killed 900,000 Europeans.

The flu epidemic of 1918–19 killed 22,000,000 worldwide, 500,000 of whom were Americans.

Tuberculosis killed 250,000 Britons between 1851 and 1855.

Insects and disease: The principal vectors (carriers) of yellow fever, malaria, and encephalitis are mosquitoes. The carrier of bubonic plague is the flea. The tick brings us typhus, Lyme disease, and Rocky Mountain spotted fever. The annual risk that you'll get Lyme disease: 1 in 120,000.

The risk that sometime during this year you will go to the doctor about

- A cold: 31%
- Flu: 38%
- An injury: 28%
- A viral infection: 9%
- Digestive tract infection: 8%
- An ear infection: 6%

On average, you'll be bedridden with one or another of these common maladies for seven days per year and will miss three days' work as a result. If you're a student, you'll miss four days of school because of illness or injury.

The risk that a case of food poisoning will be fatal: 1 in 1,000.

Where's the beef? You are 25 times more likely to get food poisoning from seafood than from beef. You are almost twice as likely to get poisoned from pork or chicken as beef. This occurs, in part, because less than 25% of domestic fish and shellfish is federally inspected. Virtually none of these inspections uses other than purely visual, naked-eye examination.

If you get influenza, your risk of dying from it: 1 in 5,000.

The two most common sources of salmonella poisoning: eating food containing eggs and handling pet turtles.

The most likely sources of rabies (in descending order of risk):

- Skunks
- Raccoons
- Bats
- Cats
- Dogs

Lest you are one of those chronic worriers about rabies, bear in mind that—media attention to the contrary notwithstanding—your chances of contracting and dying from rabies this year in the United States are less than 1 in 100,000,000. (You are much more likely to die from a plane falling on you than from rabies.)

CANCER AND HEART DISEASE

The risk that you will eventually have some form of cancer: 3 in 10.

The risk that you will be diagnosed with cancer *tomorrow:* 1 in 100,000.

If you are diagnosed with a serious cancer, your likelihood of cure: 50%.

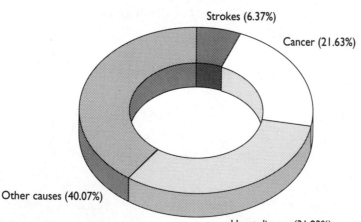

Cancer, Strokes, and Heart Disease
In Proportion to all U.S. Deaths

Strokes (6.37%)

Cancer (21.63%)

Other causes (40.07%)

Heart disease (31.93%)

The gloomiest survival rate for cancer: Only 3% of those stricken with cancer of the pancreas survive five years after diagnosis.

Blacks are twice as likely to get pancreatic cancer as whites.

The cheeriest survival rate for internal cancer: 80% of those who develop cancer of the bladder survive at least five years.

The most common cancer for a man: prostate cancer (each year 1 man in every 1,000 is diagnosed as having it).

Blacks have a *higher* incidence rate for prostate cancer than whites (almost double). Asians and Hispanics have much lower rates than whites.

The risk that a man has prostate cancer varies dramatically with his age:

- 45: 5%
- 55: 9%
- 65: 15%
- 75: 20%

The five-year survival rate for a man with prostate cancer is about 65%.

The most common cancer for a woman: breast cancer (each year 1 woman in every 1,000 is diagnosed with it).

Black women have a *lower* incidence rate of breast cancer than white women.

The risk that an American woman will develop breast cancer in her lifetime: 1 in 10.

Some details—the odds that a woman will develop breast cancer before age 70:

PANIC BY NUMBERS: BREAST CANCER

In the last several years, the media spotlight has highlighted two key facts:

Far more women die of breast cancer than ever before.

Breast cancer has moved up from third place to first among the sources of fatal cancer in women.

The unwary reader of such claims (both of which are true) is expected to come to the conclusion that breast cancer is a far more serious menace than ever. However, any panic they might cause would be unfounded—the fact is that breast cancer rates have remained essentially *constant* for more than the last half century (when adjusted for shifting ages of the female population).

The reason why more women are dying of breast cancer than ever before is simply because there *are* more women, especially older women, than ever before. Breast cancer has moved from third to first place only because the incidence of most other fatal cancers has declined.

- If there is no history of breast cancer among her immediate relatives: 7%
- If her mother had it: 12%
- If her sister had it: 13%
- If both mother and sister had it: 17%

Women who consume large amounts of vitamin A appear to run 20% less risk of breast cancer than those who consume only small amounts.

A Japanese woman is only 20% as likely to develop breast cancer as an American woman.

The odds that a woman will die of breast cancer this year: 1 in 5,000.

A woman is 170 times more likely to die of breast cancer than a man.

The five-year survival rate for a woman with breast cancer is about 70%.

Men are twice as likely to die of bladder cancer as women.

Men are also twice as likely to die of lung cancer as women.

Cancer-Producing Agents

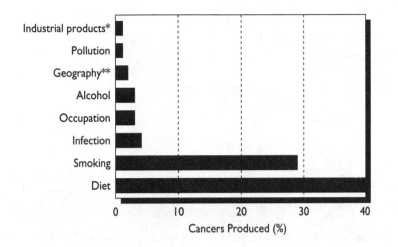

*e.g., asbestos, radium dial watches, X ray machines, etc.
**The two chief factors here are altitude (which determines the level of exposure to cosmic rays) and radon.

Radiation has been shown to be implicated in many forms of cancer. Of the radiation received by an average American each year, 82% comes from *natural* sources—radon gas (55%), cosmic rays (8%), subterranean sources (8%), and internal sources (11%).

Your risk of dying this year from lung cancer induced by radon gas (in naturally occurring amounts): 1 in 80,000.

Of the 18% of your radiation exposure that comes from *artificial* sources, more than half is from medical X rays, about 3% comes from consumer products, and less than 1% comes from nuclear fallout and the nuclear fuel cycle.

One standard chest X ray increases your chances of cancer by about 1 in 1,000,000.

If you eat 2,000 charbroiled steaks over a lifetime (say once a week during your working life), you increase your risk of cancer by 1 in 50,000.

Incidence of Coronary Heart Disese among Adult Americans

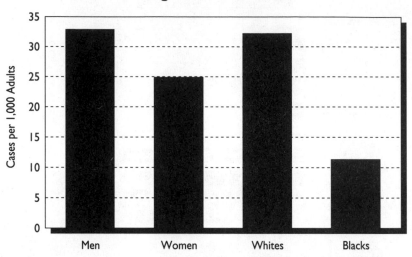

Cancer and age: A person aged 65–74 is 11 times more likely to have cancer than someone 25–34.

Very fat women are 50% more likely to develop many forms of cancer than women of average weight.

Very fat men are one-third more likely to develop cancer than men of average weight.

Another argument against the glass ceiling? White-collar men are much more likely to develop coronary heart disease than either clerical or blue-collar men. But women in white-collar jobs are far *less* susceptible to coronary disease than either clerical or blue-collar women.

White men are almost twice as likely to die of heart disease as white women.

Afro-Americans (of both sexes) are twice as likely to die of strokes as whites; black men are twice as likely as white men to die of prostate cancer.

An American woman is 6 times more likely to die of coronary heart disease than her Japanese counterpart.

An American is more than 300% more likely to die of coronary heart disease than a French citizen. In general, countries with a high per capita rate of wine consumption have low rates of fatal heart disease.

If you are over 35, your risk of having a heart attack this year: 1 in 77.

GENERAL HEALTH AND DISEASE

The proportion of Americans who will die in a health care institution: 80%. In a hospital: 60%.

More than half of U.S. women and one-third of U.S. men will spend part of their lives in a nursing home.

For the average elderly American, almost 40% of her *total lifetime Medicare expenditure* is spent during the last 30 days of

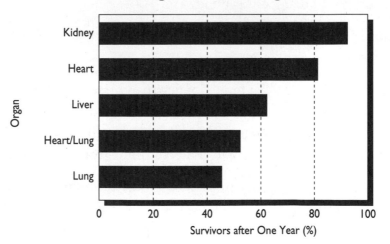

Surviving with a New Organ

her life. Almost 60% of her total expenditure occurs during the last 90 days of her life.

If you are a man, the most likely part of your body to require surgery: the digestive system. The most common type of surgery for a woman: obstetric.

Each year, for every 100 Americans, there are about 8 surgical operations requiring hospitalization.

Heroic medicine? According to a recent British study, about 1 in every 200 medical operations is performed on a patient—typically very old or very sick—whose death is deemed imminent and inevitable within 30 days, *whether the surgery is performed or not.*

The risk that sometime you will have acute appendicitis: 7%.

Removing your gall bladder is five times more likely to kill you than removing your appendix, although both are extremely low-risk procedures.

The annual risk of dying from toxic shock syndrome among women who regularly use tampons: 1 per 100,000.

Your risk of being color blind: 1 in 100.

In general, levels of health are higher in urban and suburban areas than in rural ones.

Although women live much longer than men, they tend to be sick more often. In fact, for most of the common, short-term diseases, a woman is about 15% more likely to have them than a man of her age and economic group.

Women are about 10% more likely to be hospitalized than men (even excluding childbirth) and visit the dentist about 30% more often than men.

If someone is severely burned, the probability of their dying is about the same as the percentage of the body surface affected by the burns.

The risk that a student will develop nearsightedness while attending college: 30%.

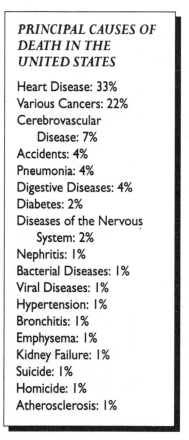

PRINCIPAL CAUSES OF DEATH IN THE UNITED STATES

Heart Disease: 33%
Various Cancers: 22%
Cerebrovascular
    Disease: 7%
Accidents: 4%
Pneumonia: 4%
Digestive Diseases: 4%
Diabetes: 2%
Diseases of the Nervous
    System: 2%
Nephritis: 1%
Bacterial Diseases: 1%
Viral Diseases: 1%
Hypertension: 1%
Bronchitis: 1%
Emphysema: 1%
Kidney Failure: 1%
Suicide: 1%
Homicide: 1%
Atherosclerosis: 1%

Widely feared conditions that probably shouldn't be: Your odds of dying this year from

- Measles: 1 in 30,000
- TB: 1 in 60,000
- Anemia: 1 in 60,000
- Hepatitis: 1 in 200,000
- Obesity: 1 in 200,000
- Appendicitis:
  1 in 500,000
- Meningitis:
  1 in 1,000,000

Anal retentives? Men are twice as likely to be chronically constipated as women.

Men are four times more likely to die of muscular dystrophy than women.

1 in every 25,000 people dies of Alzheimer's disease each year.

Up to half of those over 85 years of age are affected by Alzheimer's disease.

Contaminated blood transfusions account for about 2% of existing AIDS cases. If you receive a blood transfusion this year, the risk of acquiring AIDS is 1 in 50,000.

The risk that you will be admitted to a hospital *tomorrow:* 1 in 2,700.

Men are 90% more likely to get hernias than women. Hernias are twice as likely to be on the right side as the left.

The risk that you will suffer from mental illness at some point in your life: 1 in 5.

Women are twice as likely to be diagnosed as having a mental disorder as men are.

The risk that a black has sickle-cell anemia: 1 in 320. The odds that people with this disease know they have it: 1 in 2.

THE DILEMMA OF THE APPENDIX

The diagnosis and treatment of apparent appendicitis provides an excellent example of the sorts of risk trade-offs that this book is about. Because the symptoms of appendicitis mimic those of numerous other diseases, the doctor who diagnoses appendicitis in a patient is wrong about 20%–25% of the time.

He normally decides to operate anyway—despite knowing that he will be wrong in a sizable number of cases—because if the patient *does* have appendicitis and the doctor *fails* to remove the appendix, it may perforate, producing death in 5%–10% of the cases. By contrast, if he operates and removes the organ, the risk of death to the patient from the operation is less than 1%.

In short, it is thought to be far better to run a small risk of killing a patient who may not actually need an operation rather than to run the larger risk of failing to extract what may be an infected appendix on the verge of a potentially fatal perforation.

Risk of Common Chronic Diseases

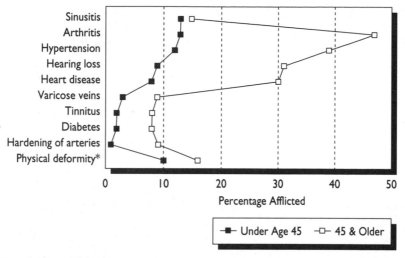

*e.g., clubfoot, cleft palate, etc.

The odds that a patient seeking admittance to a hospital emergency room has a condition genuinely requiring immediate treatment: about 1 in 2.

Among white women, X rays reveal evidence of osteoporosis with these degrees of frequency:

- Ages 50–54: 39%
- Ages 60–64: 66%
- Ages 70–74: 84%

The healthiest age group in the United States is those over 45. (Although those over 45 are much more likely to have chronic diseases, their incidence of humdrum infections such as colds, sore throat, and flu is much lower than that for younger folks.)

Among populous U.S. counties, the one with the highest (age-adjusted) mortality rate from disease is Cook County, Illinois.

Among populous U.S. counties, the one with the lowest mortality rate from disease is Los Angeles, California.

The risk that you have a high serum cholesterol level: 31%.

The risk that someone between the ages of 20 and 74 has hypertension: 51%.

The proportion of Americans in a vegetative state, with no cognitive function, kept alive by state laws prohibiting the withdrawal of life support: 1 in 17,000.

The risk that someone who has diabetes does not know it: 50%.

Your risk of getting heartburn *today:* 1 in 150.

The proportion of seafood consumed in the United States that is not inspected for disease: more than two-thirds.

The risk that a pair of breast implants will produce some complication: 2 in 5.

The risk that an adult has a food allergy: 3%.

The risk that you will develop a disability: 1 in 7.

The risk that your disability will be sufficiently serious to keep you from conducting the activities otherwise usual and appropriate to someone your age:

- Blacks: 7%
- Whites: 4%

The proportion of the U.S. population, aged 18 to 64, unable to work because of a disability: 5%.

If you are now 65 and *not* disabled, the odds are that you will be disabled for more than a third of the rest of your life.

CONCEPTION, ABORTION, AND PREGNANCY

The risk of *spontaneous* (noninduced) abortions among pregnant women: at least 15%. (It is probably much higher due to early, unnoticed pregnancies.)

The proportion of women who were ever pregnant who are known to have had one or more spontaneous abortions: 23%.

The single factor that most influences whether a spontaneous abortion will occur is the mother's age. After that, smoking and alcohol are major contributors to spontaneous abortions.

The pill and death from circulatory disease: A woman, aged 25–34, increases her chance of dying this year from circulatory disease by about 50% if she takes the pill—though even then her risk of death is only 1 in 23,000—about the same as the odds of dying this year in an accident at work. If she is

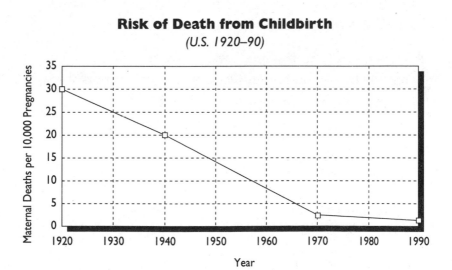

Risk of Death from Childbirth
(U.S. 1920–90)

also a smoker, she increases her risk of dying this year by 300% over smokers who do not use the pill, to about 1 in 7,000—which, although high, remains less than the risk of her dying this year in an automobile accident.

By the time a woman is 45 or over, the figures are gloomier. Pill-taking nonsmokers are 400% more likely to have a fatal circulatory disease (specific risk: 1 in 1,900) than those who don't take the pill. Worse, smokers in this age group who also use the pill stand a 1-in-500 chance of dying this year from a circulatory disease compared to the 1-in-8,800 odds among women of this age group who have not taken the pill *and* do not smoke.

Good news and bad: Pregnant women, *during* their pregnancies, are much less likely to develop serious mental illness than non–child-bearing women of the same age. However, during the six months *after* they give birth, they are slightly more likely than normal to develop serious mental problems.

The riskiest part of pregnancy for the fetus: 8–11 weeks (when 20% of all nonaborted fetal deaths occur).

A grim repetition: black fetuses are twice as likely to die before birth as white ones; black babies are more than twice as likely to die within their first month as white ones.

The risk that a random delivery in the United States will be by cesarean section: 25%. The risk in Britain of delivering by cesarean: 4%.

Pregnant women over 35 are almost twice as likely to have cesarean sections as women under 20.

The risk of twins (in normal pregnancies): 1 in 50 live births. A woman in her early 30s is more than twice as likely to have twins as a woman aged 15–19.

EXERCISE AND HEALTH RISK

A cure worse than the disease? The risk of dying during a stress test, designed to detect coronary heart disease: 1 in 10,000.

Risk that a *nonfatal* complication will develop from a stress test: 1 in 1,100.

Among regular runners and joggers, 70%–80% are hurt sufficiently badly each year to curtail or eliminate their running programs. Most likely site of injury: the knees.

> ### HISTORY IN A BOX
>
> *THE BEAT WAS HOT*
>
> Between 1989 and 1992, five people died in Manchester, England, nightclubs from "dance-floor dehydration."

The risk that a jogger will die jogging: 2.5 deaths per 1,000,000 *hours.*

Put another way, one year of jogging at least two hours a week poses a risk of dying of about 1 in 10,000.

The risk that a participant in a strenuous exercise program will die while exercising: 28 deaths per 1,000,000 hours of exercise. Such strenuous exercise for an hour a day for a year sets your risk of death from exercise close to 1 in 100.

Among soldiers aged 18–39 who died suddenly (excluding accidents and combat deaths), 57% had just completed strenuous activity, and 38% more had just completed moderate exercise.

The odds that a middle-aged businessman will develop a potentially fatal ventricular fibrillation from vigorous exercise: 1 in 10 for every 250 hours spent in the gym.

Women run approximately twice the risk of dying from heart disease during or immediately after exercise as men.

A female runner is 10% more likely to develop menstrual irregularities than a nonrunner.

The most common cause of death among marathon runners: severe coronary atherosclerosis.

The likelihood that an active jogger will die jogging this year: 1 in 7,600.

There is *no* clear evidence that strenuous exercise prolongs human life for the average person.

MALPRACTICE

The risk that an obstetrician will be sued for malpractice: 70%.

The risk that you will die this year from a misadministration by medical personnel of a general anesthetic: 1 in 1,000,000.

HISTORY IN A BOX

THALIDOMIDE

Number of children born with deformities resulting from the drug Thalidomide: 8,000.

The risk that, if you have major surgery, you will die from a general anesthetic during surgery: 1 in 25,000.

HISTORY IN A BOX

AIDS & THE BLOOD SUPPLY

Between 1978 and 1985, when testing blood for HIV+ was widely adopted by US blood banks, some 25,000–30,000 recipients were infected with AIDS. More than half the hemophiliacs receiving blood in this period developed AIDS.

The risk that you will die this year because of a "foreign object" inadvertently left in your body during surgery: 1 in 80,000,000.

According to a study by the University of Zimbabwe, approximately one-quarter of all poisoning cases in that African nation result from traditional healers' potions.

The odds that the doctor who fills out your death certificate will get the (underlying) cause of death wrong: 1 in 3.

4

The Risks of Crime

Few risks receive more media attention than crime, the single most frequent source of front-page headlines. As with disease, we are all its potential victims. It poses a threat to life, limb, and property, but not just to potential victims. There are also the risks associated with becoming a criminal (and being treated accordingly) and the risks faced by those charged with dealing with criminals (like police, judges, and wardens). The demographics of crime are hardly cheering, but in many cases the actual risks differ markedly from the popular stereotypes. Flashy crimes like sky- and carjacking or international terrorism—the sort the networks tend to serialize—are so remote as to be negligible. Real rapists are very different from the characters of pulp fiction and television docudramas. Cops on the beat lead much safer lives than you probably imagined. And our jails, far from being filled with hardened criminals, are populated in the main by arrested citizens, who are yet to be found guilty of anything.

The statistics on crime risk—more than most—are subject to debate and dispute. In part, this is because various special interest groups have a stake in their coming out one way rather than another. Exaggerating the extent of crime can serve the interests of those ardent to draw its ills to our attention. Underestimating the scope of crime, by contrast, serves the interests of others. As well, the debate about these statistics has arisen because criminal statistics, and the risk measures based on them, are drawn from law enforcement agencies, despite the fact that there are strong grounds for suspecting that many crimes (especially rape, incest, family violence, and petty larceny) go unreported to the police—perhaps by as many two crimes in three.

Federal crime authorities take measures (including extensive interviews with thousands of randomly selected citizens) to get a fuller picture than arrest dockets provide. Nonetheless, even when such allowances are made, many citizens and women's groups allege that crime in this country is vastly underestimated. That may be so. The depressing fact is that even if the official figures are on target, we are confronted by an epidemic of lawbreaking that hits, if unevenly, virtually every segment of our society.

It is impossible to discuss crime risks without using a few technical concepts of law enforcement. Hence, definitions of a few key terms are in order. As used here, the terms *theft* and *larceny* mean unlawfully taking another's property. This becomes *robbery* when it involves the use of force or the threat to use force. *Burglary* occurs when someone illegally enters a structure to commit a theft. *Aggravated assault* involves attacking another person for the purpose of inflicting severe harm; it normally includes the use of a deadly weapon. *Murder,* as used here, also encompasses nonnegligent homicide. *Forcible rape* includes all sexual intercourse without consent as well as attempted rapes but does not include so-called statutory rape (when no force is involved but the "victim" is under the age of consent). *Violent crimes* include murder, rape, aggravated assault, and robbery. *Property crimes,* as used here, refer to all serious but nonviolent crimes (like burglary, auto theft, and drug possession).

GENERAL CRIME RISKS

The rate of crime in the United States

- Every 4 seconds: a theft
- Every 10 seconds: a burglary
- Every 19 seconds: an auto theft
- Every 29 seconds: an assault
- Every 46 seconds: a robbery
- Every 5 minutes: a rape
- Every 21 minutes: a murder

During 1991, there was one serious crime for every 20 persons in the United States.

> ### QUICK OVERVIEW OF PRINCIPAL RISKS
>
> The odds that you will be a victim of these crimes this year:
>
> Murder: 1 in 11,000
> Rape (women over 12):
>   1 in 2,500
> Robbery: 1 in 429
> Assault: 1 in 261

The riskiest month for violent crimes: August (9.5%). The least risky: February (7%).

The riskiest state for violent crime is Florida, where there is one violent crime for every 84 residents. This figure may be misleading because with Florida's huge influx of tourists, its actual population at any time is much higher than its resident population, thereby reducing the per capita risk to a *resident* of being a victim of violent crime.

The riskiest month for robberies: December (9.2%). The least risky: April (7.4%).

Violent Crimes by Area

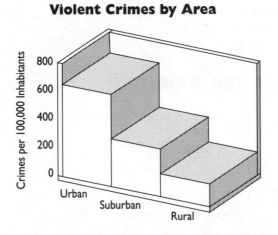

Onward Christian Soldiers—The risks to a housebreaker that homeowners of the following religious persuasions will be armed:

- Jewish: 18%
- Catholic: 36%
- Protestant: 53%

A white is three times more likely to own a gun than a black.

The risk that a burglar will have to force his (or her) way in: 43%. (Most burglars simply walk in.)

Every day in the United States, more than 100,000 students bring guns to school; every day, 40 students are hurt or killed by them.

Considering the data in the figure on page 93 and given that car thefts have very low apprehension rates, it is small wonder that motor vehicle thefts are growing faster than the rest.

The car most likely to be stolen or broken into in the United States: Volkswagen Golf. The least likely to be

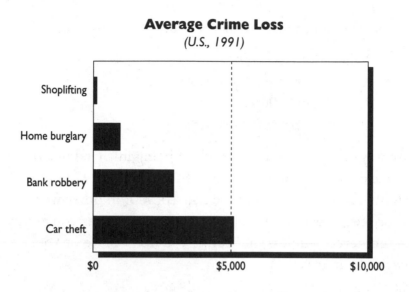

Average Crime Loss
(U.S., 1991)

stolen: Mercury Sable and Chevrolet Cavalier. (Data for 1990–92.)

The risk that, if robbed or assaulted, you'll be injured: 30%.

The odds that someone in your household will be the victim of a violent crime this year: 5%.

SAFEST AND RISKIEST MAJOR U.S. CITIES FOR VIOLENT CRIME		
Crime	**Riskiest City**	**Safest City**
Murder	Washington, D.C.	Indianapolis
Rape	Memphis	San Diego
Robbery	New York	San Antonio
Aggravated Assault	Los Angeles	San Antonio

The odds that in a given year you will be the target of

- A theft: 72 per 1,000
- A violent crime: 31 per 1,000
- Rape: 2 per 1,000
- Murder: 1 per 11,000

(By way of comparison, the odds of being involved in a traffic accident per year are 242 in 1,000. The odds of being a fatality in a traffic accident are 2 in 10,000. In other words, you're twice as likely to die in a traffic accident as you are to be murdered—unless, of course, you don't drive or you live in the inner city.)

The odds that someone will attempt to burgle your house this year: 5%.

The risk that you will be the victim of a violent crime *at work* this year: 1 in 1,000.

The poor (defined as those with family incomes less than $10,000 per year) are three times more likely to be burgled than the rich (those with yearly family incomes of more than $50,000) and are twice as likely to suffer aggravated assault.

THE WAR BETWEEN THE STATES: CRIME RATES

The per capita risk of being the victim of these crimes:

	Riskiest	Safest
Murder	District of Columbia	North Dakota
Aggravated Assault	Delaware	West Virginia
Rape	Delaware	North Dakota
Motor Vehicle Theft	District of Columbia	South Dakota

TERRORISM

The number of Americans detected every day attempting to board a plane with a firearm or explosive: 8.

The number of bomb threats to U.S. aircraft daily: 1.

The risk that an American will be killed *overseas* this year by an act of international terrorism: less than 1 in 1,000,000.

The odds that an American will be killed *in the United States* in a terrorist bombing or explosion: less than 1 in 3,000,000.

The likelihood that an attempted plane hijacking will succeed: 54%.

Your chance of receiving a live letter bomb this year: 1 in 15,000,000.

The odds that a U.S. president will be the target of an assassination attempt: 1 in 3. The risk that such an attempt will succeed: 1 in 3.

Your Risk of Homicide
Murder in Proportion to All U.S. Deaths

Homicides (1.10%)

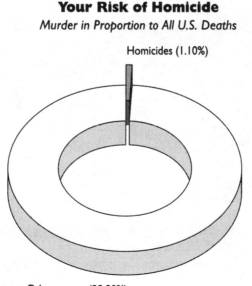

Other causes (98.90%)

MURDER

In the United States, a black is 7 times more likely to be a murder victim than a white.

Since 1950, homicide victim rates for blacks have scarcely changed at all, but they have roughly doubled for both white men and white women.

The grim reaper—The most likely day of the year for murder: January 1st.

Dutch treat: The murder rate in the Netherlands is twice that of the United States.

Homicide is the fourth leading cause of death among Hispanics in the United States. For whites, it doesn't make the top 10. (By contrast, suicide is the eighth leading cause of death among whites; it doesn't make the top 10 for Hispanics.)

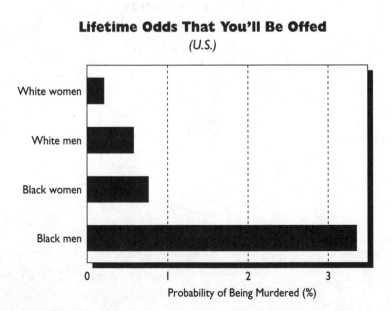

Lifetime Odds That You'll Be Offed
(U.S.)

Probability of Being Murdered (%)

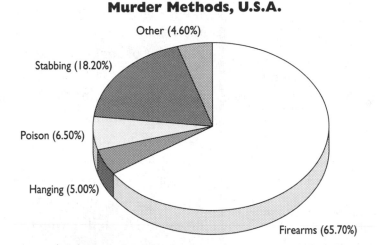

Murder Methods, U.S.A.

Other (4.60%)

Stabbing (18.20%)

Poison (6.50%)

Hanging (5.00%)

Firearms (65.70%)

HISTORY IN A BOX

WHOLESALE MURDER

Arsenic and Old Lace: The average female serial killer kills for the first time at the age of 31. She kills about 17 people, usually in her home, before she is caught. Preferred weapon: yes, arsenic. (Based on a study of about 100 cases.)

The most notorious female serial killer was probably Countess Elizabeth Bathori of Transylvania who, between 1604 and 1611, killed some 650 girls, mostly virgins.

The largest ritual sacrifice: the Aztec king Ahuitzotl celebrated the opening of a new temple by sacrificing 80,000 people at one time by the grisly method of opening their chests with a knife and removing their hearts while they were still alive.

The vast majority of U.S. murders are *intraracial.* When homicide does cross ethnic lines, it is twice as common for a black to kill a white as vice versa. (This is scarcely surprising because if a member of any minority group were to kill others purely at random, most of his victims would, of course, be from the majority group.)

The NRA's least favorite statistic—Your risk that, if murdered, the weapon will be a firearm: 66%.

It is widely believed that the ready availability of legal firearms (especially handguns) increases the likeli-

THE FLORIDA TOURISM PANIC

During 1992 and 1993, several widely publicized murders of tourists occurred in Florida, which caused several million potential visitors to that state to make other vacation plans. What went unnoted in the popular press was the fact that during the year in question, Florida had some 40,000,000 tourists, of whom 22 were murdered. Supposing that the average tourist stayed for one week, this rate is only about one-third of the average murder rate in the average American city. Being a tourist in Florida, in short, is a great deal safer than being a *resident* in most of the places whence the tourists come. Such facts made not the slightest difference to the media-fed panic about tourist risk in Vacationland.

hood that someone will commit murder, especially in a moment of anger. This is a difficult hypothesis to test, but it is worth pondering the fact that while the number of legal handguns in American homes increased by more than 10,000,000 between 1976 and 1985, the rate of spousal homicides actually fell during the same period.

The risk that someone will be shot during an armed robbery: 1 in 20.

GENDER AND CRIME

Crime and sex are multiply intertwined in modern life. Men and women commit crimes at very different rates and are victims of crime to quite different degrees. Moreover, one of the most attention-getting crimes of our age is rape, a harsh intermixing of crime and gender. If crime statistics in general tend to be suspect, those surrounding rape have become thoroughly politicized. The federal government bases its official rape figures on a combination of information gleaned from arrest dockets and from extensive random interviews with the population (so-called victimization studies).

Such official figures suggest that rape occurs perhaps twice or three times as often as it is reported.

Others, especially certain feminists, have claimed—on the basis of their own interviews and questionnaires—that there are as many as 10–15 rapes for every one reported to the police. These latter figures are suspect, because the researchers producing them work with a definition of rape that is sometimes so broad as be fatuous. For instance, some of them include—*as forms of rape*—oral sex, sex with some-one who is drunk or asleep, and even unwelcome kissing or petting. By this criterion, every woman who has ever been inebriated while having sex with her husband or boyfriend is a rape victim. As offensive as some of these activities may be, they are not *rape* as traditionally understood in law or by most of the population. By broadening the concept of rape in this fashion, one can boost the rates of its occurrence just about as high as you like.

SOME CRIMINAL DIFFERENCES AMONG THE SEXES

Men are much more likely to murder *other men* than to murder women. By contrast, women are five times more likely to kill a man than another woman.

The likelihood that a murder *victim* is male: 4 to 1.

The ratio of males to females shown being killed in television programs and movies: 200 to 1.

The proportion of male to female murderers: 9 to 1.

For most age groups, men are more than three times as likely as women to be the victims of violent crimes.

Murder Victims, by Sex
(U.S., 1991)

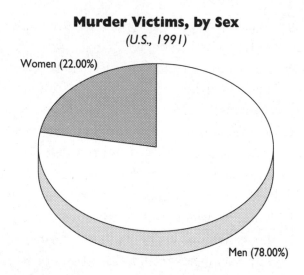

Women (22.00%)

Men (78.00%)

Divorced or separated women are 60% more likely to be victims of violent crimes than married women.

Never-married women are 500% more likely than their married counterparts to be victims of violent crime. (Coincidentally, never-married men are the most likely perpetrators of violent crime.)

Divorced or separated women are 400% more likely to commit violent crimes than married women.

Divorced or separated men are 300% more likely to perform violent crimes than married men.

In case you doubted the reality of premenstrual stress syndrome (PMS), ponder the fact that the *majority* of crimes committed by women occur during the week before menstruation. (Mere chance would obviously lead us to expect about a quarter of crimes to be committed then.)

In *every* major category of crime except prostitution, women have a lower per capita arrest rate than men.

RAPE

The risk that a woman's rapist is a stranger: 2 out of 3. The risk that a burglar is a stranger: 2 out of 3.

The official risk (based on police reports) that a woman under 30 years of age will be raped in a given year: 2 per 1,000. If she is white: 1 per 1,000.

Lifetime risk of a black woman being raped: 1 in 9. A white woman: 1 in 13. (Assuming that about half of committed rapes go unreported, the previous four risk figures should all be doubled.)

A poor woman (in a family with a yearly income of less than $10,000) is 20 times more likely to be raped than a rich woman (in a family with a yearly income of more than 50,000).

A woman aged 16–19 is nine times more likely to be the victim of a violent crime than a woman over 65.

Rape in Proportion to All Violent Crime in the United States

Rape (5.30%)

Other violent crime (94.70%)

> **PROFILE OF THE AVERAGE RAPIST:**
>
> A stranger to the victim
> Acting alone
> Same race as the victim
> Early 20s
> Unarmed
> Unmarried

The chance that a rapist will use a weapon: 20%. When a weapon is used, a knife is more common than a gun. (Similarly, a knife is the weapon of choice in robberies.)

The odds that a person arrested for rape is a woman: 1 in 78.

A woman in Houston or Los Angeles is more than twice as likely to be raped this year as her counterpart in Philadelphia.

The riskiest time of day for a rape attempt: 6 P.M. to midnight (37% of rapes occur in this 25% of a 24-hour day).

A woman is 20% more likely to be raped in the summer than in the winter.

Where Rape Occurs

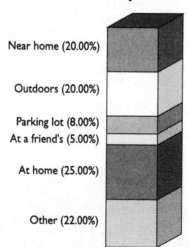

Near home (20.00%)

Outdoors (20.00%)

Parking lot (8.00%)
At a friend's (5.00%)

At home (25.00%)

Other (22.00%)

Campus rape: During 1991, the two U.S. campuses with the highest number of known rapes were the University of Michigan and Michigan State University (9 each).

> **PROFILE OF THE MOST-AT-RISK RAPE CANDIDATE:**
>
> Under 25
> Poor
> Black
> Unmarried
> Away from home in the evening

The risk that a rape will involve more than one offender: 15%.

The risk that a rape will involve more than one acquaintance or friend: 1.5%.

Proportion of rape complaints deemed false or baseless by law enforcement agencies: 8%. (The average number of criminal complaints of all types determined to be unfounded: 2%).

Rapists of white women are four times more likely to be white than black.

Rapists of black women are eight times more likely to be black than white.

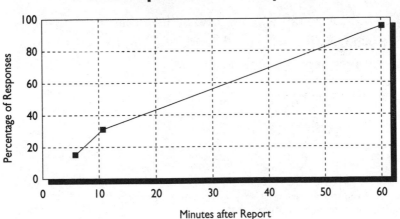

Police Response Time to Rape Calls

Hispanic men are more likely to rape white women than fellow Hispanics.*

Judging by recent patterns, Hispanics are twice as likely to be arrested for rape as whites; blacks are six times more likely to be arrested for rape than whites, and Asians are 60% *less* likely to be arrested for rape than whites.

A white woman is three times more likely to be raped than an Hispanic woman.

According to police officials, the proportion of consummated rapes reported to the police: 65%. The proportion of *attempted* rapes reported: 24%.

The risk that an attempted rape will succeed: 51%.

Among those rapes that are reported to police, almost a quarter are reported *more than four weeks after their occurrence,* making successful prosecution of the rapist—even if he is apprehended—very difficult, due to the lack of physical evidence.

Of women who took protective measures during a rape, the percentage who subsequently believed that these measures helped: 55%.

The proportion of women who believe that the availability of pornography increases the risk of rape: 68%. The number of men who share that opinion: 49%.

The risk of being raped in the United States is

- Twice that of Canada

---

*One should not read more into this statistic than is on the surface. To stress a point made earlier: If a member of a minority commits crimes *at random* on passersby, it will inevitably turn out that most of the victims of that minority criminal are members of the majority.

- Three times that of England, Germany, Sweden and Denmark
- Five to ten times that of France, the Netherlands, and Japan

The demise of the dirty old man myth: A woman is more likely to be raped by a boy between the ages of 10 and 12 (4% of the male population) than by a man aged 65 or older (12% of the male population).

Attacks with a deadly weapon (aggravated assault) occur 39 times more often than rape.

For a woman, the risk of being the victim of an aggravated assault with a deadly weapon is 4–5 times greater than the risk of rape.

Apart from being much more frequent than rapes, aggravated assaults with a deadly weapon are much more likely than rapes to produce serious injuries requiring hospitalization.

It may, then, come as a bit of a surprise that criminals convicted of rape generally receive *longer* prison sentences than those convicted of attempted murder, armed robbery, or assault with a deadly weapon.

If that seems slightly askew, ponder as well the fact that the minimum sentence for possession (not sale) of a modest amount of LSD (10 years) is almost twice as long as the minimum sentence for a rape conviction (5.8 years).

The most common age for

- Prostitutes: 23
- Rapists: 22
- Vehicle thieves: 16

ALL IN THE FAMILY

Parents are 50% more likely to use violence on their children than vice versa.

Even so, you are 50% more likely to be treated violently by your siblings than by your parents.

THE RISK OF FAMILY VIOLENCE IS GREATER WHEN

The man is less educated than the woman

The couple are blue-collar workers

The man is unemployed

The family's income level is low

The couple are not legally married

The couple are black

The man's job status is lower than the woman's

The percentage of U.S. marriages with at least one instance of violence between spouses: 60%.

The risk that a married couple will at some time engage in some form of *serious* physical violence toward each other: 25%.

Battered wives and husbands occur in roughly equal numbers. Debate rages about how many of the husband-batterings are retaliatory or self-defense.

A married black (male or female) runs roughly twice the risk of being the victim of spouse abuse as a married white. (When adjusted for family incomes, these figures move much closer together.)

Murder within the family:

- Husbands are twice as likely to kill their wives as vice versa
- Children murder their fathers more often than their mothers

- Parents murder their sons more often than their daughters
- Brothers are murdered five times more often by their siblings than sisters are

Clearly, the safest niche in the family—at least where homicide is concerned—is that of daughter/sister.

A romantic triangle is much more likely to be the occasion for murder within the family than disagreements over money or property.

If you are murdered, there is a 1-in-8 chance that the murderer was a member of your immediate family. There is a 1-in-3 chance that the murderer was a friend or acquaintance. This adds up to a slightly better than 50–50 chance that the murderer was a stranger.

THE CRIMINALS

Who are they? Most of us! 90% of all men and 65% of all women report that they engaged in some form of illegal activity in childhood or adolescence.

The risk a criminal runs that her crime will be reported to the police: 1 in 3.

The percentage of criminals in federal prisons who are charged with *drug* offenses: 43%.

The percentage of prison inmate deaths due to AIDS: 17%.

The proportion of deaths of inmates in local jails due to AIDS: 10%.

The risk that a New York City prison inmate is HIV+: 20%.

The proportion of prison inmate deaths due to suicide: 6%.

The proportion of jail inmate deaths due to suicide: 43%.

In most states, what determines whether a convicted adult felon goes to jail or prison is the *length* of the sentence. (Generally, terms of a year or longer are spent in prison; shorter sentences, in jail.)

The risk that a randomly selected American is currently in jail, prison, on probation, or on parole: 1 in 40. However, this figure varies widely, depending on locale; for a randomly selected resident of Washington, D.C., the risk is 1 in 20; for a randomly selected resident of North Dakota, it's 1 in 170.

The proportion of Americans admitted to local jails each year: 4%.

The proportion sent to state and federal prisons each year: 0.2%.

The risk that a man will end up in prison sometime in his life: 1 in 40.

A black man runs a 600% greater risk of going to prison than a white man.

The risk that a white woman will serve a prison term: 1 in 700.

The risk that a black woman will go to prison: 1 in 100.

The majority of jail and prison inmates have never been married.

The likelihood that a New York City arrestee will test positive for cocaine use: 75%.

The revolving jailhouse door? The risk that a young parolee will be back in prison within six years of release: 50%.

Persons aged 16 to 21 are three times more likely to be arrested than those of other age groups.

THE MEN (AND WOMEN) IN BLUE

How much protection have you got? The number of police officers per 1,000 population

- In Washington, D.C.: 6.2
- In San Antonio and San Diego: 1.5

The number of police officers per square mile

- In New York City: 91
- In Kansas City, Missouri: 3

Hollywood's least favorite crime statistic: The risk that a randomly selected police officer will be slain this year in the line of duty: 1 in 3,100. (The risk of a farmer or miner being killed on the job this year: 1 in 2,300.)

Friendly fire: Roughly half of all police officers wounded in the line of duty are shot accidentally by a fellow officer.

The risk that a New York City traffic officer will be physically assaulted this year: 1 in 12.

The odds that a New York City policeman will fire his gun in the line of duty this year: 1.5%.

In large U.S. cities, your risk of being arrested by a police officer who is

- Male: 91%

- Black: 14%
- Hispanic: 8%

THE CRIMINAL JUSTICE SYSTEM

The number of arrests in the United States per year: about 14,000,000.

The percentage of people in jail who have been *convicted* of a crime: 49%. Those awaiting trial or arraignment account for the remaining 51%.

The average prison sentence for a convicted rapist: 15+ years.

The average prison sentence for someone convicted of second-degree murder: 15 years.

The risk that someone arrested for rape will be jailed *without bail:* 5%. That is, 95% of accused—but not yet tried—rapists are set free, provided they can raise bail.

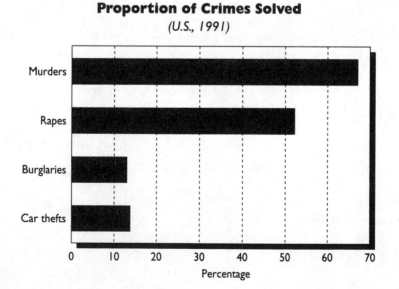

Proportion of Crimes Solved
(U.S., 1991)

AVERAGE PRISON SENTENCE (IN YEARS), ACCORDING TO METHOD OF TRIAL			
Crime	**Jury**	**Judge**	**Guilty Plea**
Murder	28.4	20.8	14.3
Rape	17.7	13.0	10.7
Drugs	7.8	10.2	4.9

Innocent until proven guilty? The risk that a defendant in a Japanese criminal trial will be found guilty: 99%. In the United States: 60%.

If you are convicted of homicide, the chances of your not going to prison: 12%.

If you are convicted of rape, burglary, or robbery, the chances of not going to prison: 21%.

For every 100 persons accused of committing a felony and recommended for trial by the police:

- 45 cases are dismissed before trial
- 52 plead guilty
- 3 are tried, 1 of whom is acquitted and 2 of whom are found guilty

Of these 54 convicted felons, 32 are sentenced to jail, while 22 are put on probation. The striking figure here is that although 54% of accused felons

TOUGHER JUDGES ... FEWER CRIMES?

Those who believe in deterrence hold that being tough on criminals will lower the crime rate. They might ponder the fact that the United States has a higher proportion of its population behind bars than any other industrial democracy. That notwithstanding, we continue to have the highest rate of crime.

go to jail, only 3 out of those 100 accused felons actually go to trial.

The risk that someone charged with murder will be released on bail, pending trial, within 2 days or less of their arrest: 40%.

A convicted murderer risks execution by firing squad only in Utah; he can be hung only in Montana and Washington.

HISTORY IN A BOX

PUBLIC EXECUTION.

During the Reign of Terror following the French Revolution, 60 people per day were publicly beheaded by guillotine.

The risk that a request for a Presidential Pardon will be denied: 9 in 10.

An Officer and a Gentleman? In the U.S. Army, an enlisted man or woman runs a 1,000% greater risk of facing court-martial than an officer.

In the U.S. Air Force, enlisted personnel are three times more likely to be court-martialed than an officer.

5

The Risks of Sin

This chapter covers the classic Victorian sins of the flesh: sex, booze, drugs, tobacco, and gluttony. For all their prudery about these matters, however, it seems that the Victorians were not very successful at avoiding them. Syphilis and gout, for instance, were chronic nineteenth-century disorders. So was alcoholism. The historical record suggests that as far as such naughty indulgences are concerned, few of us are willing to swear off altogether. This persistent fact perplexes public health officials who understand that the wages of sin are sometimes death and disease; having realized that they cannot outlaw sex, they content themselves with urging its sanitized practice. Similarly, with gross over-eating, the authorities have placed their bets on an informational campaign as the best way of drawing our attention to the relevant risks.

With drugs, however, and increasingly with tobacco and alcohol (which are, after all, drugs as well), public health authorities have become increasingly aggressive. Illicit drug use has long been a target of the federal government, especially since the 1930s—the stepped-up campaign against drugs coinciding fortuitously with the end of Prohibition, when thousands of government liquor control agents were on

the verge of losing their jobs. Tobacco appears to be the official vice of choice for lawmakers during this decade, with a
new assault on alcohol probably to come early in the next
century.

What lies behind all this government interest is the simple fact that sex with multiple partners, smoking, drinking,
overeating, and using drugs are risky things to do. Whether
people continue to do these things because they are unaware
of the risks or whether any risks are outweighed by the plea-
sure is unclear. Thus, there is nothing preachy about the data
presented in this chapter. They are meant simply to inform
you of the levels of risk associated with the pleasures of the
flesh.

SEXUALLY TRANSMITTED DISEASES

This section deals with the risks of syphilis, gonorrhea, and
AIDS. Although all three diseases can be transmitted through
nonsexual contact, they are classified as sexually transmitted
diseases because that is their principal mode of transmission.

The proportion of Americans in 1991 with

- AIDS: 1 in 5,700
- Gonorrhea: 1 in 450 (among blacks, 1 in 67)
- Syphilis: 1 in 5,800

(Recent broadening of the official definition of AIDS would
increase its rate slightly.)

You run the greatest risk of contracting syphilis in Mississippi, where 1 in 2,100 adults has it. The smallest risk is in
North Dakota where, apparently, no one has it.

The risk of contracting syphilis in the United States is only
one-third what it was in 1950.

THE WAR BETWEEN THE STATES: OCCURRENCE OF NOTIFIABLE DISEASES

The frequency of disease per capita:

	Riskiest	Safest
AIDS	Washington, D.C.	North Dakota
Gonorrhea	Washington, D.C.	Vermont
Syphilis	Washington, D.C.	North Dakota
Measles	California	North Dakota
TB	Washington, D.C.	Wyoming

Having unprotected sex just once with someone who has a venereal disease poses a risk of roughly 30% that you will become infected. The risk is greater from syphilis than from gonorrhea.

In the United States, a black is three times more likely to have AIDS than a white.

A white man is seven times more likely to have AIDS than a white woman.

A black man is four times more likely to have AIDS than a black woman.

Among white men in the United States, about three-quarters of the cases of AIDS diagnosed between 1983 and 1989 resulted from same-sex contacts.

From 1983–89, the majority of U.S. men with AIDS were white; the majority of women with AIDS were black.

Male AIDS sufferers outnumber females by about 8 to 1.

About 1-in-4 AIDS victims has acquired it from intravenous drug use.

Less than 1 white woman in 150,000 currently dies each year of AIDS. (This is about the same level of risk as that of choking to death on food lodged in the throat.) Less than 1 white woman in 43,000 contracts AIDS each year.

Slightly more than half of all U.S. AIDS victims are male homosexuals or bisexuals.

At its *peak,* the polio epidemic of the late 1940s and early 1950s killed about 3,000 persons per year in the United

---

SAFE SEX?

Of the 950 white women who contracted AIDS in the U.S. in 1989, fewer than one-third acquired it from heterosexual contact, and the majority of those cases involved contact with an intravenous drug user. In sum, among the roughly 76 million white American women between the ages of 15 and 65—supposing all of them to have been sexually active— the frequency of contracting AIDS from a year's worth of sexual liaisons was about 1 in 250,000. If none of their partners shoots drugs, the frequency drops to less than 1 in 500,000. (That means that if you are a member of this group, your risk of contracting AIDS is less than the risk of accidentally electrocuting yourself.) Even if we were to suppose that only half of the women in this age group had a sex partner in 1989, the risk is still very low.

Among white *men* who avoid sex with IV drug users, about 1 in 1,000,000 develops AIDS from a year of heterosexual contacts. (Obviously, the risks increase as the number of sexual contacts grows.)

Either everyone is using condoms, sex has been abandoned on a massive scale, or the risk of AIDS from *heterosexual* encounters is more remote than some would have us believe.

States. The AIDS epidemic kills more than seven times that number every year.

If that figure underscores the seriousness of AIDS, it puts a slightly different twist on it to realize that the average American is about as likely to be murdered as to die from AIDS.

The riskiest city for AIDS: Newark, New Jersey (1-in-75 adults there has it).

Nationwide, AIDS is the leading killer of black men ages 25–44; it is the second-leading killer of white men in that age group.

The median age of AIDS victims: 36.

The risk of contracting AIDS from *one* heterosexual encounter with an HIV+ partner:

- Without a condom: 1 in 500
- With a condom: 1 in 5,000

A woman is more than twice as likely as a man to contract AIDS from one sexual encounter with an infected partner of the opposite sex.

Of those Americans who died of AIDS between 1984 and 1990, about 2% of the male victims and almost 33% of the female victims contracted AIDS through *heterosexual* encounters.

CONCEPTION AND CONTRACEPTION

A sexually active, fertile woman's risk of getting pregnant this year if she uses no method of contraception: 4 in 5.

Failure Rates of Contraceptives

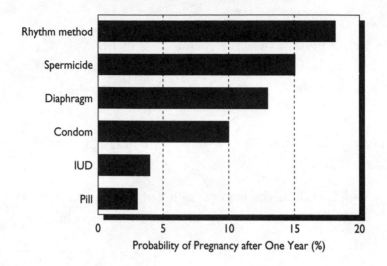

Probability of Pregnancy after One Year (%)

Each occasion of unprotected sex between a fertile, healthy couple of childbearing age poses a 5%–10% risk of pregnancy. If sex continues, the risk that this couple will conceive within one year: 85%–90%. If they have sex four or more times per week, the prospects of pregnancy increase to 97%.

Condoms reduce that risk to 0.5%–1.0% per occasion. The rhythm method reduces it to about 2% per occasion. Intercourse once (or more) a week using the rhythm method makes it more likely than not that a woman will be pregnant within three years.

The what-to-make-of-it department: Widows and divorced or separated women are more likely to use the IUD than are married women.

No Mensa members here: About 8% of fertile, married couples who do *not* want a child claim to be using *no* method of birth control.

The solution to sluggish sperm? Caffeine in the bloodstream (from coffee or tea) increases the mobility of sperm in the vaginal tract by several hundred percent.

The risk of pregnancy this year for a woman who takes the pill faithfully: 1 in 1,000.

The risk of pregnancy if she takes it less than faithfully: 1 in 20.

The percentages of married women of childbearing age who practice some form of contraception:

- British: 83%
- Canadian: 73%
- American 68%
- Chinese: 7%

The odds that a married American woman, aged 15–45, is *not* on the pill: 4 to 1.

The risk that regular use of the pill will kill a nonsmoker this year: 1 in 80,000.

Regular use of the birth control pill apparently decreases the risk of ovarian and endometrial cancer.

The pill is the contraceptive of choice among Protestant and Catholic women. The condom leads among Jewish women.

The wish as father (or mother) of the deed: It seems that the effectiveness of a contraceptive method depends, in part, on the mind set of the woman using it. For instance, among women who were using contraceptives to *prevent* pregnancy, the failure rate was about 3%–4%. But among women who were using contraceptives merely to *delay* pregnancy, the failure rate was 7%.

By age 44, 61% of American couples have been sterilized (meaning that at least one member of the pair has been sterilized).

The risk that a couple, between the ages of 25 and 35, will be involuntarily infertile: 1 in 7.

ABORTION

The odds that a child resulted from an *intended* pregnancy if his or her parents were married at the time of conception: 65%.

The proportion of *unintended* pregnancies by a married couple that are also *unwanted*: 1 in 3. This means that 1-in-9 pregnancies within marriage are unwanted. Because the marital abortion rate is lower than this, it is clear that a small fraction of these babies come into the world unwanted.

Women favoring a woman's right to an abortion: 65%. Men favoring it: 70%.

The abortion rate in New York state is eight times greater than in Wyoming.

The risk that a randomly selected woman between the ages of 15 and 44 will have an induced abortion this year: 1 in 34. (The rate for Washington, D.C.: 1 in 7.)

Most women receiving an induced abortion (58%) have never had one before.

Less-than-true believers: Most of the world's major religions—Judaism, Roman Catholicism, Protestantism, Islam, and Hinduism—take a dim view of the termination of unwanted pregnancies. Nonetheless, women of all those faiths have induced abortions in almost the same numbers as those who profess no religion.

Number of medically supervised abortions for every 100 live births:

- Among whites: 25
- Among blacks: 46

Russia has an abortion rate 5 times higher than the United States. India, on the other hand, has an abortion rate 20 times smaller than the United States'.

Among married women, there are 8 abortions per 100 live births; among unmarried women, there are 88 per 100 live births.

The risk for Americans of living in a county in which no legal abortions are performed: 82%.

The odds that an abortion will be performed in a hospital: 1 in 9.

Given a sample of 100,000 women, all of whom are sexually active, healthy, of reproductive age, and not using any form of contraception, at least 50,000 would probably be pregnant within a year. The odds are that if all those pregnancies were aborted medically before the ninth week of pregnancy, less than one of those women would die as a result. If, on the other hand, *all* continued with their pregnancies, then three or four women would be likely to die from complications.

The *lowest* rates of abortion are among the least educated (8 years of schooling or less) and the most educated (16 years or more).

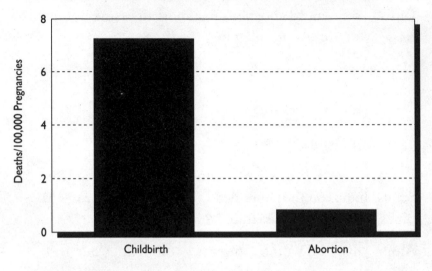

The Relative Risks of Abortion v. Childbirth

White married men, aged 15–44, are 1,300% more likely to have had a vasectomy than black married men. By contrast, black married women of that age group are 66% more likely to have been sterilized than white married women.

BOOZE AND ILLICIT DRUGS

The proportion of U.S. adults who drink: 2 in 3.

Recent estimates suggest that the use of alcohol, tobacco, or illicit drugs is implicated in about one-quarter of all deaths in the United States.

The average American consumes 3.3 liters of spirits (alcoholic beverages other than wine or beer) each year. Contrary to popular impression, Russian consumption is no higher. Germans, on the other hand, consume twice this quantity.

The average American consumes 8.3 liters of wine each year. The Portuguese consume 11 times that amount.

If a man and a woman of the same age and weight drink the same amount of alcohol, the woman's blood alcohol concentration will be higher than the man's.

That is probably why, among heavy drinkers who consume the same quantities of alcohol (relative to their weight), women are more likely than men to develop cirrhosis of the liver.

The risk of a man developing cirrhosis of the liver from drinking three ounces of alcohol (equivalent to about four beers or four shots of whiskey) daily or less: negligible. Women, by contrast, increase their risk of cirrhosis by consuming as little as one ounce per day.

Even so, a man is four times more likely to die from cirrhosis of the liver than a woman.

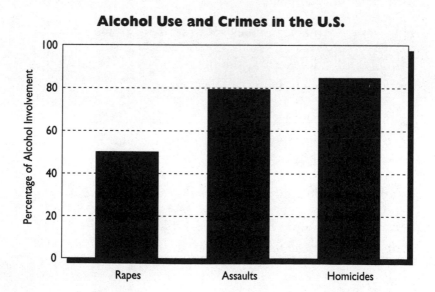

Alcohol Use and Crimes in the U.S.

Men are three times more likely to die of alcohol and drug dependency than women.

Your odds of becoming an alcoholic this year: 1 in 1,500.

A person's chances of a successful and permanent treatment for alcoholism are less than 1 in 4.

An alcoholic is about 400% more likely to die this year than a nondrinker of the same age and sex.

Almost half of all murder *victims* had been drinking immediately before they were killed. Whether it was their drinking that made them more likely to be murdered or whether they were drinking because they anticipated what was coming is unclear.

Female alcoholics are three times more likely to suffer premature death than nonalcoholic women.

All things in moderation: Women who have one or two drinks each day are likely to live longer than teetotaling women of the same age.

The average American takes his first drink at age 12.

Among U.S. adolescents, the percentages of those who report having been drunk at least once:

- 8th graders: 18%
- 10th graders: 40%
- 12th graders: 53%

Alcohol is implicated in 44% of all accidental deaths.

Among drivers aged 21–24 involved in fatal traffic accidents, 35% were legally intoxicated.

Alcohol's double-whammy: Everyone knows that if you drink and drive, you are more likely to have a fatal accident because of impaired motor skills. Less widely appreciated is the fact that if two drivers—one who has consumed a lot of alcohol and one who has not—sustain chest injuries of the *same* degree of severity, the drunk is much more likely to die from that injury than the nondrinker.

An alcoholic is likely to die 12 years sooner than his nonalcoholic cohorts.

The risk of dying from alcohol-related causes, if you are an alcoholic, is about twice as great as the risk of a regular smoker dying from tobacco-related diseases.

Among those aged 18–25, slightly more than half report the use of one or another *illicit* drug. In most cases, the drug in question is marijuana.

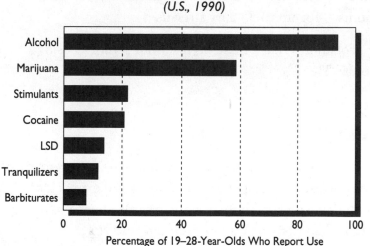

Drug Use by Young Adults
(U.S., 1990)

Percentage of 19–28-Year-Olds Who Report Use

The risk that a person admitted to an emergency room for a drug overdose will die: 3%. The drug most commonly responsible for overdose cases seen in emergency rooms: alcohol.

The risk that a first-time user will become addicted to

- Cigarettes: 9 in 10
- Crack cocaine: 1 in 3

Losing the battle? Between 1988 and 1992, the feds more than doubled the budget for the "war on drugs." (We currently spend more than $50 annually for every person in the United States on combatting drugs.) In that same period, the number of drug-related emergencies treated in hospitals increased by more than 10%, and the number of drug users contracting AIDS from shared needles increased more than 50%.

An *undisputed* danger of pot: Most commonly used drugs wash themselves out of the system within 72 hours after use. Marijuana stays in the urine—in readily detectable amounts—for up to *35 days* after use.

The probability that a male high school senior is using steroids: 2%–3%.

SMOKING

Among men, smokers are twice as likely to die prematurely as nonsmokers. More generally, if you smoke a pack of cigarettes a day, you run about a 70% greater chance of dying this year than nonsmokers of your age and sex.

The proportion of cancer deaths linked to smoking: 30%.

Most people (roughly four out of five) who get lung cancer are smokers or former smokers. All the same, most smokers and former smokers never develop lung cancer. (About 1 in every 250 smokers or former smokers develops lung cancer each year.)

Among nonsmokers, men are 30%–50% more likely to develop lung cancer than women. But among heavy smokers, women *may* run twice the risk of lung cancer that men do. (This latter claim is still contested by some researchers.)

Cigarette smokers have a higher incidence than nonsmokers of cancers of the lung, larynx, esophagus, bladder, pancreas, kidney, and lip.

Smoking two packs of cigarettes daily is 10 times more life-threatening than usual levels of cigar smoking and 14 times more dangerous than usual levels of pipe smoking.

Smokers are 1,000% more likely than nonsmokers to develop chronic emphysema and chronic bronchitis.

White men and women smoke cigarettes in roughly equal numbers. Black men are 50% more likely to smoke than black women.

The risk that you will develop a fatal cancer this year caused by exposure to secondary tobacco smoke: 1 in 80,000. (This is roughly the same risk as that of dying from accidental poisoning.)

Those teenagers who try smoking are 16 times more likely to smoke as adults than those who do not.

Women who smoke are likely to have menopause 1–2 years earlier than those who don't smoke.

Older smokers have a *lower* rate of Alzheimer's disease than nonsmokers of comparable ages.

A smoker is twice as likely to commit suicide as a non-smoker.

The average American consumes more than 2,500 cigarettes each year. Because most do not smoke at all, the use of cigarettes among smokers themselves is more than double this figure.

Your odds of stopping smoking on the first attempt: less than 20%.

Many smokers will attempt to stop but fewer than 50% will succeed, even after repeated attempts.

Smokers who quit smoking before age 50 run only one-half the risk of dying in the next 15 years as those who continue smoking.

Longtime smokers who quit gain about 5 pounds on average; 1-in-20 quitters gains 20 pounds. (See the next section to find out what *that* does to your chances of living to a ripe old age!)

The state with the highest per capita loss of life due to smoking: Kentucky. The state with the lowest loss of life: Utah, where fewer than 1-in-7 adults smokes.

Men are most likely to smoke in Alaska. Women are most likely to smoke in Nevada. Although men are generally more likely to smoke than women, Oregonian women out-smoke their male counterparts.

EATING

Obesity increases your risk for

- High blood pressure
- High cholesterol levels
- Coronary heart disease
- Uterine and breast cancer
- Gall bladder disease
- Diabetes

How risky is your weight? There's a simple calculation: Being 7% overweight will probably shorten your life by about a year. If you are 14% overweight, then your life will lose an average of two years. As obesity increases beyond this level, the effects are even more vivid than a simple extrapolation of these figures would suggest.

The grossly fat (those who are 100 pounds or more over their ideal weight) are 50% more likely to die in a given year than persons of the same age and sex who are the "ideal weight."

The risk that an American woman, aged 20–74, is obese: 28%.

Obesity among men aged 20–74 tends to be fairly uniform among the races (about 25% of the male population is significantly overweight). Among women, however, there are more dramatic variations; fewer than 20% of Hispanic women are obese, while almost 44% of black women fall in that category.

The average American consumes 64 pounds of fat and oils and 65 pounds of sugar each year.

A high-salt diet increases the risk of high blood pressure and strokes.

Bad diets probably produce even more cancers than cigarette smoking does.

The risk that someone with acute anorexia nervosa will die of the disease: 18%.

6

Risks from Nature and Technology

We live in an age when *natural* has come to mean "benign" and anything made, created, or devised by humans seems both artificial and suspect. Such attitudes have spawned some of Madison Avenue's greatest oxymorons. (My personal favorite: The instant coffee that is "naturally decaffeinated.") The chemophobes among us would have us believe that chemistry itself is a purely human concoction— as if there were no chemical elements and compounds, no pollutants, and no poisons before modern science began fabricating them. As the data in the first half of this chapter will make clear, the natural and the benign are not necessarily the same thing.

Nature does loads of nasty things to us. Floods, storms, earthquakes, hurricanes, volcanoes, and tornadoes are just the tip of a very jagged iceberg. Most diseases are natural. Most naturally occurring substances are poisonous. The single largest source of cancer-producing radiation is radon gas, a byproduct of the decay of radioactive elements in the earth's crust. Also implicated as sources of cancer-causing radiation are cosmic rays and ordinary sunlight. Indeed, death itself is as natural as can be. If we have been able to prolong life beyond its traditional span of three score years and ten, that is because we have been clever enough to contrive ways of delaying the decay, disease, and destruction that is inflicted on us by nature.

Think about it another way. All plants, including those we eat, contain many *naturally occurring pesticides.* They have evolved these toxic—in many cases, carcinogenic—defenses against insects and other predators over millions of years. It has been estimated that we consume 10,000 times as many natural pesticides as artificial ones. So is nature really so benign? Other numbers give this question further punch. It is a widely used rule of thumb among risk specialists that, in any given year, about 30 times as many people will die in natural disasters as in man-made ones.

Nature's onslaughts notwithstanding, there are still plenty of ways in which our technological society poses major threats to our lives and health, especially through damage to the environment in which we live. Some of these ways are described below. But if you read carefully, you will find that many things commonly regarded as environmental risks (like carbon monoxide emissions or sulfur oxides) are not included here. This is in keeping with a promise I made in the first chapter to discuss only those risks that we know how to quantify and to express with precision.

The unhappy fact is that we have some grounds for thinking that many air and water pollutants may be risky, but we have as yet no dependable data on the *size* of the risk they pose. In other words, although we have a pretty good idea of the amount of the principal pollutants released into the air and water in the United States, there are very few studies on the health effects of specific concentrations of particular pollutants. Such studies are fiendishly difficult to perform because there are too many variables outside our control. Is a certain oxide of nitrogen dangerous in a particular amount? Usually the answer is, We do not know.

Because, as I said earlier, everything is risky, it is meaningless to be told that this or that pollutant poses a "potential" risk—until we know what the magnitude of the risk is. Unless we know whether a certain pollutant in certain concentrations kills (say) 5,000 people a year or 1 person every decade, we cannot decide whether it poses an unacceptable risk. And because scientists have generally not yet been able to identify the size of many of the risks posed by most of the pollutants in the environment, I devote scant attention to them here.

In fact, such studies as there are raise doubts about the commonly assumed risks of some pollutants. In New York City, for instance, levels of sulfur dioxide fell more than 90 percent between 1969 and 1976 in response to the Clean Air Act of 1970. Despite this drastic shift in one of the most common air pollutants, daily mortality rates in New York did not change at all. No doubt New York City smells better, but it is unclear whether *any* lives were saved by the curtailment of sulfur emissions.

The problem of assessing environmental risks is made worse by the official doublespeak on the subject that emanates from Washington. Consider but one example. From time to time, a federal agency will announce that it has identified a certain substance (natural or artificial) as a "*possible* human carcinogen." Such announcements are generally greeted with much wringing of hands from the general public, who suppose that one more item must be struck off their menus or life-styles. The facts, however, are quite otherwise. To qualify as a possible human carcinogen, there must be evidence that the substance in question produces cancer in rodents when they receive doses of the substance that are often a million times stronger than a human being receives, even allowing for differences in body weight. Even if we suppose that the likelihood of cancer varies directly with the level of exposure and that whatever is carcinogenic to rodents is dangerous to humans (and both assumptions are dubious), these figures mean that the likelihood of a human being getting cancer from normal exposures to the substance is about a million times smaller than the rat's chances. If you reflect on the other risk statistics in this book, it will become clear that such risk is extraordinarily low—in fact, it is about as close to "safe" as we normally get in this life. Accordingly, the discovery that something is a *possible* human carcinogen (given the curious way the feds define this term) is the discovery that—except for the pathologically risk-averse person—it may be *less* harmful than many of the things we routinely do. (*Known* human carcinogens are in a different class.)

A different sort of example is provided by the notorious chemical dioxin (an ingredient in Agent Orange of Vietnam War fame). Dioxin is a common byproduct of many industrial processes, and federal standards dictate that there be less than 15 parts of dioxin per quintillion parts of drinking water. That amounts to less than one *drop* of dioxin in a reservoir the size of Lake Michigan. Put another way, it is equivalent to one second of time in 2,000,000 years. Needless to say, reducing dioxin levels that low is a very pricey business. The irony is that this highly expensive standard is strictly enforced and dioxin's killer reputation remains nearly universal, despite the fact that the 100-odd studies on dioxin's effects on health have failed to exhibit *any* significant carcinogenic effects for human beings.

NATURE DOING NASTY THINGS TO US

The number of Americans killed by lightning in 1989: 700. Your risk of dying from lightning this year:

- For men: 1 in 2,000,000
- For women: 1 in 10,000,000

Your risk of being injured by lightning tomorrow: 1 in 250,000,000. Your risk of being injured by lightning sometime during your life: 1 in 9,000.

Worldwide, about 44,000 thunderstorms and 9,000,000 lightning flashes occur daily.

The riskiest month for lightning in the United States: July. The riskiest state for lightning: Florida.

Half of all forest fires are started by lightning.

Deaths Due to Acts of Nature
Relative to All Accidental Death

Nature (1.20%)

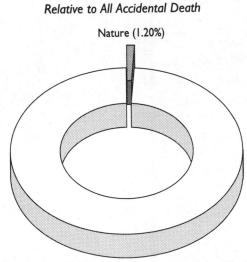

Other causes (98.80%)

Californians take heart: Judging by recent experience, you are even less likely to die from an earthquake than from lightning.

And now for the bad news—The risk of a quake measuring 7.0 or greater on the Richter scale in southern California before September 1, 1997: 47%. The risk of such a quake within the next year: 5%–12%.

Although most of us think of California, Hawaii, or Alaska as the likely sites for large quakes, the fact is that very large earthquakes (Richter magnitude 8.0 or greater) have occurred in these other states during the last two centuries:

- Arkansas (2)
- Illinois (2)
- Indiana (1)
- Kansas (2)
- Michigan (2)
- Missouri (2)
- Ohio (3)
- Tennessee (1)
- Texas (1)

Several of these areas are regarded as overdue for the next tremor.

A tornado hits the United States about twice a day on

NATURE'S FURRY CREATURES

Animals pose a variety of risks to humans. Here are a few:

One of the principal causes of salmonella poisoning is the handling of pet turtles.

Almost one in every five fatal farm accidents is caused by an animal.

Your lifetime risk of being seriously bitten by a dog: 45%.

Your risk of being seriously bitten by a cat: 5%.

About 25% of the world's diseases fatal to humans are carried by insects; another 6% are carried by other mammals, especially rodents.

The proportion of U.S. children that sooner or later require hospital treatment for bee or wasp stings: 37%.

EARTHQUAKES, VOLCANOS, AND TIDAL WAVES

The worst urban earthquake on record shook Shaanxi, China, in 1556, killing 830,000 people.

America's worst urban quake was the 8.3-magnitude giant that struck San Francisco in 1906. Deaths: 503. Duration of the quake: 2 minutes.

Who's counting? In 1811 and 1812, there were numerous earthquakes near New Madrid, Missouri, some of them actually shifting the course of the Mississippi River. Between December 16, 1811, and February 7, 1812, New Madrid residents recorded 1,875 tremors—roughly 35 quakes per day.

The worst U.S. tidal wave struck Hilo, Hawaii, in 1946, killing 179 people.

In 1896, a tidal wave struck Japan and killed 28,000.

The worst volcanic disaster in recorded history was the eruption on April 11, 1815, of Mount Tambora in Java, which killed 94,000 in its vicinity and countless others by virtue of producing worldwide cold weather and famine during 1816. (By comparison, the Mount St. Helens eruption in 1980 killed 61.)

average. The risk that a particular tornado will kill someone: 1 in 100. Your risk of dying from a tornado this year: less than 1 in 2,000,000.

Your risk of being injured by a tornado this year: 1 in 200,000.

The riskiest month for tornadoes: May.

The safest place in your house when a tornado hits: the closet. The safest part of your house: the center or the northern side—not, as in popular folklore, the southwest corner.

The poverty factor: If you live in a rich country, your chances of dying in a natural disaster are about 10% as great as the chances of those living in poor countries.

Your risk of dying this year from an impact with a meteorite: about 1 in 5,000,000,000.

The odds that if a meteor were to hit the United States, it would land on one of our cities: 1 in 1,000. The most likely cities to be hit: Honolulu or Houston. (No mystery here—they happen to be the cities with the greatest area in the United States.)

Tidal waves (or *tsunamis*), typically caused by earthquakes under the oceans, are walls of water (often 20–30 feet high) moving at speeds of up to 500 miles per hour.

HISTORY IN A BOX

WIND AND WATER

The worst U.S. tornado roared across Missouri, Illinois, and Indiana on March 18, 1925, killing 689 people.

The most disastrous flood on record occurred along the Huang He River in China in 1931, killing 3,700,000 people.

During one particularly heavy snow storm in Sweden in 1719, more than 7,100 travellers died before they could reach safety.

A hailstorm in India in 1888 killed 250 people.

The worst hurricane on record slammed Bangladesh on November 13, 1970, killing 300,000 people. The worst U.S. hurricane struck Galveston, Texas, in 1900, resulting in 6,000 deaths.

Every surfer's dream, every sailor's nightmare: Leaving aside tidal waves, there is enormous variation in the height of waves due to such factors as wind patterns. Once every month, at any given spot in the sea, there will be a wave that is four times higher than normal. These can sometimes be killers. In the North Atlantic, for instance, any given spot well away from land will receive a 70- to 80-foot wave approximately once a year.

You are three times more likely to be killed by a rainstorm than a blizzard.

Of those who die in floods in the United States, 74% perish in cars that are washed away.

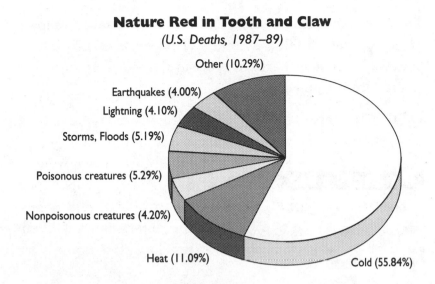

Nature Red in Tooth and Claw
(U.S. Deaths, 1987–89)

Other (10.29%)
Earthquakes (4.00%)
Lightning (4.10%)
Storms, Floods (5.19%)
Poisonous creatures (5.29%)
Nonpoisonous creatures (4.20%)
Heat (11.09%)
Cold (55.84%)

You are twice as likely to die from excessive cold as from excessive heat. Your risk of freezing to death this year: 1 in 3,000,000.

Close to home: The risk that your county will suffer a tornado, major flood, or hurricane within a decade: 37%.

The riskiest place for volcanoes: the Philippines, with more than 100 active ones. Japan and the Aleutians come next, with 33 and 32 active vents, respectively.

Ice ages generally last about 100,000 years, interrupted by warm periods of about 10,000–20,000 years. Our current warm cycle is about 10,000 years old. According to some scientists, the risk of a new ice age starting within the next century: 1 in 10.

When the next ice age comes, these countries are likely to be *wholly* obliterated by ice sheets: Canada, Ireland, United Kingdom, all of Scandinavia, Nepal, and New Zealand.

The likely number of deaths due to ice sheets and accompanying droughts: 2,000,000,000. (The droughts will arise because on a colder Earth, less ocean water will evaporate to produce precipitation.)

On the other hand, if the global climate warms rather than cools, thus melting the polar ice caps, sea level could rise about 24 feet, which would wipe out a large proportion of the world's current population centers. In the United States alone, this would mean the disappearance of all or parts of

- Baltimore
- Boston
- Honolulu
- Houston
- Jacksonville
- Long Beach
- Los Angeles
- Miami
- New Orleans
- New York City
- Philadelphia
- Portland
- San Diego
- Virginia Beach
- Washington, D.C.

Residents of places like Denver or Mexico City are exposed to at least double

---

HISTORY IN A BOX

CLIMATE AND FAMINE

The highest recorded temperature on Earth: 136°F at El Azizia, Libya (1922).

The lowest recorded natural temperature on Earth: −129°F at Vostok, Antarctica (1983).

The greatest recorded rainfall in:

- One minute: 1.23 inches at Unionsville, Maryland (1956)
- 24 hours: 74 inches at La Reunión Island (1952)
- One year: 87 feet at Cherrapunji, India (1860–61)

The Maryland record is equivalent to receiving about 150 feet of rain in one day!

By contrast, Arica, Chile, had no rainfall whatever for almost 15 years between October 1903 and January 1918.

A severe drought produced a famine in China from 1876 to 1879 that killed more than 13,000,000 people.

the amount of cosmic radiation that people living at sea level receive.

Those who regularly drink soft water run a 15% greater risk of cardiovascular disease than those drinking hard water.

Radiation from *natural* (as opposed to artificial) sources accounts for more than 80% of the radiation to which we are normally exposed. It follows that most of the cancers produced by radiation are also "natural."

Your risk of dying this year from lung cancer induced by radon gas (in naturally occurring amounts): 1 in 80,000. Making your home more energy efficient (in other words, more of a radon trap) increases this risk accordingly.

These counties produce the highest level of air pollution:

- Carbon monoxide: Denver County, Colorado
- Lead: Collin County, Texas
- Nitrogen dioxide: Davidson County, Tennessee
- Ozone: Los Angeles County, California
- Particulates: Imperial County, California
- Sulfur dioxide: Lee County, Iowa

Extraterrestrial (and thankfully, rare) natural events that might do us all in:

- A nearby star (less than, say, 50 light-years away) could suddenly become a supernova, thus producing levels of cosmic rays on Earth equivalent to the explosion of tens of thousands of H-bombs. The likelihood of occurrence: 1 per 1,000,000,000 years.
- The Earth's magnetic field vanishes to nothing roughly every 200,000 years, possibly exposing life to high

levels of ultraviolet radiation. The last such event occurred some 600,000 years ago. Some scientists believe that we are overdue.

- A mini–black hole could explode in the vicinity of the Earth, annihilating all life. No one knows whether such objects of the physicist's imagination are lurking nearby.
- Comets collide with the Earth about once every 100,000,000 years raining devastation (but not total obliteration) in their wake.
- Asteroids hit the Earth about every 250,000 years, producing craters up to 12 miles in diameter and causing dramatic short-term climatic effects.

ARTIFICIAL RISKS AND DISASTERS

The proportion of U.S. dams located at sites where, if they failed, there would likely be loss of life: 40%.

HISTORY IN A BOX

DAM FAILURE

The worst U.S. dam collapse occurred in Johnstown, Pennsylvania, in 1889, claiming 2,200 lives.

Your risk of dying this year from the failure of a dam: 1 in 10,000,000.

It is generally estimated that the ozone layer is being depleted at the rate of about 5% per decade. Based on the worst estimates, your added ultraviolet exposure each decade as a result of this process is roughly equivalent to what you would experience if you were to move some 100 miles towards the equator. Put differently, a *century* of such ozone depletions would produce levels of ultraviolet exposure in New York City roughly equivalent to those now routinely experienced in Miami.

It is likely, however, that even that statistic is an exaggeration of the actual effects. For instance, a five-year study recently concluded in Britain found that although there was an 18% decrease in the ozone layer over Britain, the levels of cancer-causing solar radiation reaching the ground actually *fell* rather than increased during that period. Some scientists now believe that *natural* fluctuations in the sun's output of energy may be much more important than changing ozone concentrations in determining how much damaging radiation reaches the Earth's surface.

The risk that at least one U.S. nuclear reactor will have a core meltdown within the next 20 years: 1 in 8.

The risk posed by the entire U.S. stockpile of high-level nuclear wastes, provided we can agree on an underground depository to put them in: one death per decade for 10,000 years. If they are *not* buried, the risk they pose is, of course, much greater.

The risk to life run by those who live near a nuclear plant is about the same level of risk as that posed by eating two teaspoons of peanut

---

HISTORY IN A BOX

CHERNOBYL

The accident at the nuclear plant in Chernobyl in April 1986 killed 31 people immediately.

The long-term fallout: Soviet radiation experts estimate (and Westerners generally agree) that the nuclear accident at Chernobyl will cause cancer deaths to increase as follows:

- About 4%–7% over the next 70 years for those then living within 20 miles of the site

- About 0.07% over the next 70 years for those living in Europe and what was the western Soviet Union

The accident at Chernobyl released 3,000,000 times as much radiation into the air as Three Mile Island did.

Estimated *long-term* effects of the release of radiation in the Three-Mile Island affair: 2 deaths. (There were no short-term fatalities.)

HISTORY IN A BOX

THE BHOPAL DISASTER

The leakage at the Union Carbide
plant in Bhopal, India, in
December 1984

- Killed more than 2,500
  immediately

- Increased the spontaneous
  abortion rate in the vicinity from
  2% to 14%

- Afflicted several tens of
  thousands with disabling lung
  and eye problems

butter daily. (Peanut butter
contains aflatoxin, a rodent
carcinogen.)

Your lifetime risk of dying
from exposure to *all* forms
of air pollution: 1 in 30.

79,000,000 or so Americans
live in counties with levels
of ozone in the air that
exceed EPA standards; about
61,000,000 live in counties
with excessive carbon
monoxide.

The odds that a Russian lives where air pollution exceeds
"safe" levels by 500% or more: 3 to 1.

According to the EPA, 80% of U.S. coastal waters are able
to safely support wildlife and human recreation. 56% of
rivers and streams can provide clean drinking water.

HISTORY IN A BOX

URBAN POLLUTION

An episode of smog in London
between December 5 and
December 8, 1952, killed more
than 7,000 people.

The risk that a randomly
selected U.S. public water
system contains what the
government regards as "dangerous" amounts of lead:
20%.

The amount of lead contam-
ination in drinking water caused by the dissolution of lead in
faucets: 20%.

The risk that the water from your tap is not chlorinated:
20%. (If you are a chemophobe, I should probably put

it this way—the risk that you are drinking chlorinated water: 80%!)

Lifetime risk of cancer from exposure to airborne asbestos fibers: 1 in 250,000 (rural outdoors) to 1 in 25,000 (urban outdoors).

The risk of dying from pesticide poisoning this year: 1 in 200,000 (worldwide).

The risk that an underground well contains potentially harmful levels of pesticides: 1 in 10.

The risk that *bottled* drinking water bought in the United States is contaminated with bacteria: 30%.

According to the U.S. Food and Drug Administration, the following are the principal hazards to health in the foods we eat (in descending order of threat):

- Microbiological contamination
- Industrial or natural pollutants

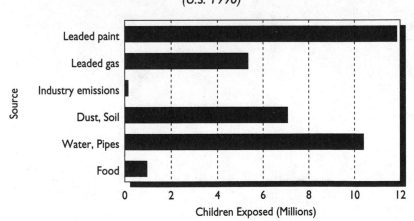

Significant Lead Exposure during Childhood
(U.S. 1990)

- Naturally occurring toxins in foodstuffs
- Pesticide residues
- Food additives

Microscopic organisms, as opposed to chemicals, account for more than 95% of all food-related diseases.

The estimated number of underground gasoline tanks in the United States leaking petroleum products into the soil: 10,000.

The odds that a given oil tanker will have a serious discharge of oil this year: 2%.

The proportion of oil moving through U.S. waters that is spilled: 0.05% (about 10,000 tons per year).

The proportion of this loss that double-hulled vessels would prevent: 50%.

Each year, between 3,000,000 and 5,000,000 metric tons of oil drain into the Earth's oceans.

7

A Miscellany of Risks

This chapter is about a diverse assortment of killer risks chiefly having to do with general mortality, childhood, suicide, and war.

THE GRIM REAPER

Mortality tables are the tools of statisticians and actuaries. In dry and digested form, they present a vivid history of human sex and death, and like much else in this book, they give the lie to the claim that we are all the same. The facts of mortality vary dramatically according to sex, class, ethnicity, and geographic region. If the proverbial three score years and ten is the age to which we normally live, the fluctuations around that figure are both wide and deep.

The single most striking discrepancy is, of course, between the life spans of men and women. As of 1993, life expectancy for women was 6.9 years longer than for men in the United States. This gender-based difference in mortality is generally more pronounced than any of the racial or economic differences between us. (For example, white women live 5.1 years longer than black women.) But those economic and ethnic differences, as some of the numbers on the fol-

Human Longevity
(U.S., 1850–1990)

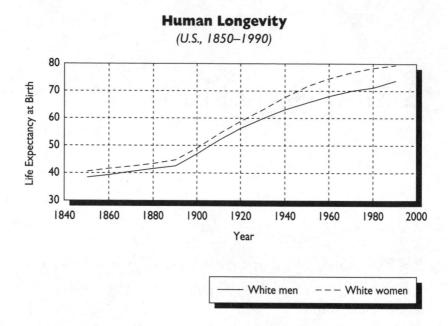

lowing pages indicate, are far from minor. If being female confers the largest advantage where mortality is concerned, income level and race are close contenders. Indeed, one of the largest risks you could run—after being born male—is being poor. That trait alone is far more likely to kill you than smoking, drinking, hereditary disease, or life-style. If, besides being poor, you are also black and male, then this particular combination probably costs you about 20 years of longevity, compared with a well-heeled, white woman.

The one aggregated risk we all face: An American dies every 15 seconds.

Under the age of 65, blacks and American Indians have the highest death rates; Asian Americans have the lowest.

The odds that a Native American will die before reaching 45: 1 in 3.

A baby born in 1993 in the United States can expect to live 75.5 years.

The chances that you'll still be living with your spouse (though not necessarily your *present* one) at ages 75–84:

- Men: 71%
- Women: 28%

The most likely month for dying: January. The least likely month: September.

The odds that you will die without ever having been married:

- Men: 12%
- Women: 8%

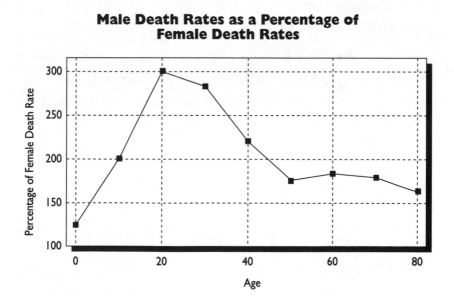

Male Death Rates as a Percentage of Female Death Rates

The odds that if you are now married, you will have no living spouse when you die:

- Men: 40%
- Women: 72%

A 50-year old man has a 4% chance of dying before 55. A 50-year old woman has a 2% chance of not making it to 55. At 60, *he* has a 9% chance of dying before 65; *her* odds—5%.

At age 85, a white woman would find that 40% of her white childhood girfriends were still alive. Only 21% of her white boyfriends and 28% of her black girlfriends would still be around. A scant 13% of her black boyfriends would have survived.

If you are a man aged 60 or over, your odds of dying in the three hours it takes to read this book: about 1 in 150,000.

The most likely day of the week to die: Saturday.

A man aged 15–24 is 300% more likely to die than a woman of the same age.

The average woman born in 1900 could expect to live less than three years longer than her male counterpart. By 1990, a newborn female could expect to outlive her male twin by about 7 years. In sum, although longevity has increased during this century for both men and women by almost a quarter of a century (on average), the gap between male and female life expectancy has increased almost 300%.

Blacks, male and female, are 50% more likely to die this year than their white counterparts of the same age.

THE WAR BETWEEN THE STATES: PRINCIPAL CAUSES OF DEATH

The risk per capita of dying from diverse causes:

	Riskiest	Safest
Heart Disease	Pennsylvania	Alaska
Cancer	Washington, D.C.	Alaska
Accidents	Alaska	New Hampshire
Suicide	Nevada	New York
AIDS	Washington, D.C.	North Dakota

A resident of Washington, D.C., is 290% more likely to die this year than someone living in Utah.

Blacks under 35 are twice as likely as whites to die by gunfire.

The average Japanese boy born in 1987 will live four and one-half years longer than his American contemporary. The average Russian boy born in 1987 will die more than six years earlier than his American contemporary.

A Hungarian is twice as likely to die this year as an Australian.

Between 1900 and 1975, U.S. rates of premature death (from all causes) were cut in half. Since 1975, however, they have changed scarcely at all.

Are we really living so much longer? The average white male who was 60 in 1850 could expect to live another 16 years. His counterpart in 1992 can expect to live another 19 years.

This many animals are known to be threatened with extinction:

- Mammals: 698 species
- Birds: 1,047 species
- Reptiles: 191 species
- Fish: 762 species
- Invertebrates: 2,250 species

CHILDREN AT RISK

However carefree childhood sometimes appears, it carries its share of risks, not least because those are the years when you work your way through childhood diseases, learn how to play the game by society's rules, and begin to explore the outer envelope of risky activities. Each of the various phases of childhood has its own risk profile. The chief risk factor during the first year of life is disease, when people run a higher

Childhood Deaths

in Proportion to All U.S. Deaths

Ages 0–14 (2.60%)

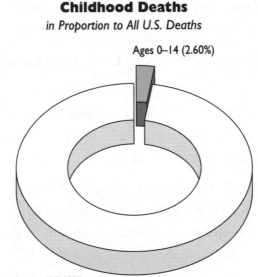

Ages 15 and over (97.40%)

risk of fatal disease than they will until they reach the age of 65. This is also the riskiest period of life for being a murder victim. Entering the 1–14 age group marks a transition to life's low-risk phase. Those in this age group have a lower rate of death than any other ages. On the side of nonfatal risks, however, this is when children are most likely to begin a life of crime and when they are most likely to be abused by their parents. For the 6–14 age group, the most dramatic fatal risk exposure is from drowning. Between 15 and 19, risk exposures rise dramatically, as accidents, homicide, and teenage suicides begin to exact a high toll.

INFANCY

The risk that a baby will be murdered *before it is two months old:* 1 in 15,000. (For the sake of comparison, the homicide risk for an adult during a two-month period is about 1 in 60,000.) This brief window involves the highest exposure to homicide—typically committed by a parent or close relative—in the individual's life. Incredibly, homicide ranks as the fifth leading cause of death for very young infants.

An infant is three times more likely to be injured in a high chair than in a playpen.

The use of a child restraint device reduces the chances of fatal injury to an infant under 1 year old by about 70%.

In New York City, AIDS is the leading cause of death of children between the ages of 1 and 4.

The risk that a baby born to an unmarried woman will be given up for adoption:

- White: 17%
- Black: 1%

The odds that a child selected at random was adopted: 1 in 140.

The odds that a child, whose parents were married when it was conceived, was the result of an *intended* pregnancy: 65%.

The riskiest part of pregnancy for the fetus: 8–11 weeks (when 20% of all noninduced fetal deaths occur).

There are 32 countries (including Cyprus, Costa Rica, and Jamaica) where a newborn can expect to live longer than in the United States. Even so, the rate of infant death in this country is less than half what it was only 20 years ago.

Black infants, compared to white ones, are at least twice as likely to die during their first year from

- Influenza
- Pneumonia
- Low birth weight
- Respiratory Distress Syndrome
- Sudden Infant Death Syndrome (SIDS)
- Accidents
- Homicide

Boys, of all races, are 25% less likely to reach their first birthday than girls.

Over the hump: The risk of a 28-day-old infant dying before its first birthday is only 10% what it was when he or she was born.

An American boy, aged 1–4 years, is twice as likely to die as his Swedish counterpart.

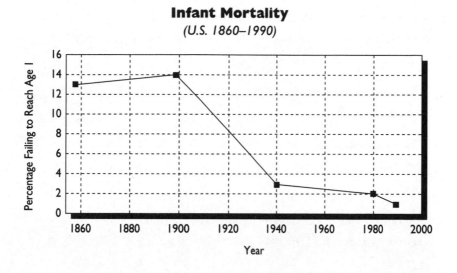

Infant Mortality
(U.S. 1860–1990)

Since 1975, the American Academy of Pediatrics has insisted that there is no medical rationale for circumcision. Notwithstanding, the risk that a newborn American boy will be circumcised: 60%. The risk that a British boy will be circumcised: 11%. (The AAP recently reversed itself.)

Baby boys have more fatal congenital anomalies than girls.

The risk that a baby will be of low birth weight:

- White: 7%
- Black: 13%

The risk that a baby will not survive until its first birthday:

- White: 1 in 125
- Black: 1 in 54

The risk that a baby will die in its first year from Sudden Infant Death Syndrome (SIDS): 1 in 700. This represents

14% of all infant deaths. As usual, boys are more than twice as likely to suffer it than girls. The riskiest time for SIDS: the third month of life.

The risk that a newborn baby will have a serious birth defect: 1 in 6.

The risks of an American infant dying from all causes in 1990 were less than 10% what they were for a child born in 1915.

The odds that a baby will be delivered by someone other than a physician: 1 in 29.

The risk of a Down's syndrome birth: 1 in 600.

The odds that a boy will be hemophiliac if his mother is a carrier: 1 in 2.

48% of all drowning deaths occur among those under the age of 5.

The sickliest group in the United States is those under the age of 5.

CHILDHOOD

More than 50% of childhood deaths result from injury rather than disease.

The proportion of hospitalizations of children due to toy-related injuries: 5%.

The odds that a child admitted to a hospital because of poisoning will die: 1 in 250.

Fewer than 1 child in 10,000 will die from cancer this year.

So much for that man's-best-friend nonsense—the risk that a child will at some time be bitten by a dog: 45%.

Boys are bitten by dogs twice as often as girls. To preserve the asymmetry, it is also true that male dogs bite children more often than bitches do.

By contrast, female cats are twice as likely to bite humans as toms are, and they principally bite girls. A child's risk of being bitten by a cat this year: 1 in 1,600.

If a child is hit by a car moving at these speeds, his or her risk of death:

- 40 mph: 70%
- 30 mph: 50%
- 20 mph: 5%

Children are 600% more likely to be killed *by* a school bus hitting them than they are to be killed while travelling *on* the school bus.

Nightmare on Elm Street—the odds that a child riding a school bus will be injured this year: 1 in 7,000.

Mile for mile, a school bus is much more likely to be involved in an accident than a car. However, mile for mile, the risk of injury or death to a child in that bus is less than to a passenger in a car by a factor of 16 to 1. The moral here is that a child is more likely to be injured in an accident in a bus than in a car, but he is a great deal more likely to walk away from a bus accident.

A diphtheria epidemic in 1931 killed 17,000 American children. The disease killed none in 1988.

The lifetime risk that a child, exposed for five years at school to commonly occurring levels of asbestos fiber, will acquire a fatal asbestos-linked cancer: 1 in 2,500,000.

If a child spends grades K–12 in a school building containing asbestos fibers in ceilings or insulation, her *lifetime* odds of getting a fatal asbestos-linked cancer increase to 1 in 170,000. (You may well wonder why schools are being required to spend billions of dollars annually to clear away all asbestos.)

The risk that a child will develop leukemia this year: 1 in 20,000.

The risks of being a victim of sexual abuse as a child:

- Girls : 10%
- Boys: 5%

The average age of victims of sexual abuse: 9.3 years.

The likelihood that the sexual abuser of a child is his or her parent: 56%.

The odds that a child will be seriously abused or neglected

- In Missouri: 60 instances per 1,000 residents
- In Pennsylvania: 7 instances per 1,000.

The risk that a sexually molested child will still claim to be carrying the emotional scars of the ordeal as an adult: 15%.

A child is more likely to be physically abused by the mother (94% of mothers physically abuse their children) than by the father (65%).

The risk that a child will be spanked by his parents: 90%.

The risk that a parent will be physically abused *by his or her children* 18 and under this year: 10%.

The risk that a runaway child will become a prostitute: 10%.

A black child is four times more likely to have "dangerous" levels of lead in her blood stream than a white child. (I have put quotations around the word *dangerous* because there is much controversy as to whether lead exposure really has acute health hazards at the levels now defined as threatening by the federal government.)

The weapon of choice in childhood suicides: firearms (56%), except among American Indians, for whom hanging is the clear favorite.

A young child in an infant seat strapped to the front seat so as to face the rear of the vehicle could be killed or seriously injured by an activated air bag.

If you are 19 or under and a licensed driver, your chances of having an accident this year: 28%.

If you are 19 or under and a licensed driver, your risk of being involved in a *fatal* accident: 1 in 1,500.

Those aged 19 and under constitute about 5%–6% of licensed drivers. They are involved in more than 12% of fatal accidents.

SUICIDE

Suicide, according to the dictionary, is willfully killing yourself. The statistics on suicide place it among the top 10 killers of Americans (specifically, number 8). But those statistics are themselves suspect as understating the dimensions of the problem. For a variety of understandable reasons, especially in a society where doing yourself in is a criminal act, relatives and family physicians have a clear motive for finding other official causes of death when confronted by an apparent suicide. There is also a conceptual problem with figuring out when to view a death as a suicide. For instance, is someone who willfully engages in highly risky activities really committing suicide? Say, someone who drives while heavily intoxicated or a three-pack-a-day smoker? What about a boxer or the pilot of a private plane? When these people die "doing their thing," should we call it suicide? Much probably depends on that elusive element, intent. Many people engaging in high-risk activities, even when they know the danger involved, suppose that it will be "the other guy" who loses to the odds. Is this genuine self-deception or simply an excuse? The answers are rarely clear-cut.

Suicides in Proportion to All U.S. Deaths

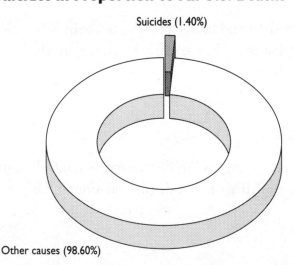

Suicides (1.40%)

Other causes (98.60%)

The following figures about suicide finesse all those subtle questions by simply supposing that a suicide is someone who deliberately and knowingly engages in an action that is overwhelmingly likely to terminate his or her life.

You are marginally more likely to kill yourself than to be murdered by someone else. A suicide occurs in the United States approximately every 20 minutes.

The risk of an American dying by suicide this year: 1 in 10,000. However, the risk is 1 in 5,000 among men; for women, the risk is 1 per 20,000. That is, men commit suicide about 400% more often than women.

Among white Americans, suicide ranks as the fourth leading cause of death when severity is measured using a YPLL scale (see Chapter 3 for a discussion of YPLLS).

Suicide rates for white men have increased about 10% in the last 40 years; they have dipped about 5% for white women. During that same period, black male and female suicide rates have increased about 50%. However, it remains true that whites are far more likely to kill themselves than blacks.

The preferred age for suicide shows a bizarre variation with both race and sex. White men have their highest annual rate of suicide (0.7%) over the age of 85. White women (0.08%) and black men (0.2%) are most likely to kill themselves between the ages of 45 and 54. Black women have their highest suicide rate between the ages of 25 and 34 (0.04%).

The likelihood that a Kuwaiti will commit suicide: 1 in 1,000,000.

The risk that someone who *threatens* to commit suicide will actually do it: 1-in-10.

Suicide Sequence—Chances the Average American Will. . .

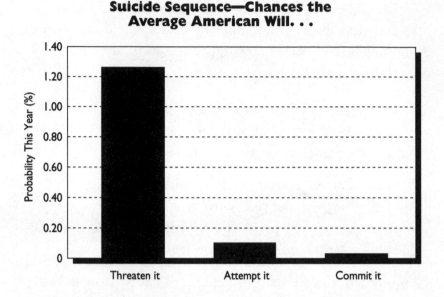

Among those aged 20–24, a Japanese man is 1,100% more likely to commit suicide than his American counterpart. A Japanese woman of that age group is 1,600% more likely to commit suicide than her American cousin.

Lest you still subscribe to the (Scandinavian) theory that cold climes, grey skies, and maudlin personalities are a major cause of suicide, ponder the fact that the supposedly dour Scots have far lower rates of suicide, among both men and women, than Americans.

Sore losers? Residents of Nevada are 350% more likely to commit suicide than residents of nearby New Mexico.

A smoker is twice as likely to commit suicide as a non-smoker.

Suicide epidemic? In the two months after Marilyn Monroe's suicide in 1962, the national suicide rate increased roughly 25%.

Preferred Method for Ending It All
(U.S. 1991)

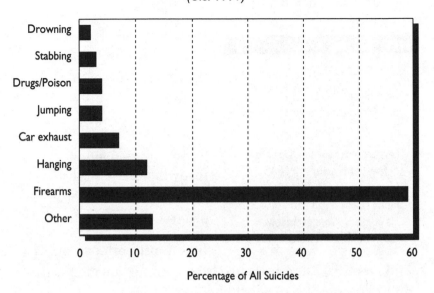

Percentage of All Suicides

The riskiest month for suicide: March. The least risky: December.

Esprit de corps? Members of the armed forces are 300% more likely to commit suicide on the job than civilian workers.

There has been a marked movement away from poison and knives and toward the use of firearms in suicide attempts. This is bad news for health officials, because a firearm is a much surer way of accomplishing the job than slashing your wrists or taking a fistful of aspirin.

The suicide rate for American Indians (1 in 5,000) is almost twice that for whites, which in turn is twice that for blacks.

Men are seven times more likely than women to commit suicide at work.

If you are a divorced white man, you are four times more likely to commit suicide than if you are married. If you are a divorced white woman, you are three times more likely to do yourself in than if you are married.

Widowers are 40% more likely to commit suicide than married men of the same age.

Only 1-in-50 suicides occurs in the classic manner of throwing oneself off a bridge or some other high place.

If you lost both parents as a child, you are 700% more likely to commit suicide as an adult than someone who still has both parents.

The mentally ill are 1,500% more likely to commit suicide than the general population.

Temporal lobe epileptics are 2,500% more likely to commit suicide than the general population.

WAR

The risk that nuclear weapons are deployed in your state: 50%.

During World War I, more than 90% of the 7,000,000 men who served in the armed forces of Austria-Hungary were either killed, wounded, or taken prisoner. Three-quarters of the Russian army in that war met the same fate.

During the month-long Battle of Verdun (February 1916), more soldiers—chiefly French and German—died than the

United States has lost in *all* wars since its founding. On several horrific days during that battle, *daily* casualty figures were greater than the *total* U.S. battle losses during the Vietnam War.

It is usually true that far more men are wounded in battle than are killed. During World War II, however, nine times as many Japanese soldiers were killed as wounded.

During World War II, a U.S. merchant seaman was much more likely to die from enemy action than his counterpart in the U.S. Navy or Army.

In Vietnam, a U.S. Marine was 3 times more likely to die than someone in the U.S. Army and 19 times more likely to die than a sailor in the U.S. Navy.

The number of wars (defined as prolonged conflicts between organized armies) worldwide between 1945 and 1992: 120.

Since the close of World War II, wars have killed more than 6,000,000 soldiers and 9,000,000 civilians.

An additional 6,000,000 people have died as a result

HISTORY IN A BOX

WAR AND MEDICINE

World War II was the *first* war in history in which a U.S. soldier was more likely to die from wounds on the battlefield than from other causes (chiefly disease).

In one particularly striking case of the impact of disease on war, Sir Francis Drake lost about 100 men to battle during the roughly two weeks that his fleet spent fighting the Spanish Armada. He lost more than 3,000 men to food poisoning.

Real-life M.A.S.H.—the time delay in various wars between a soldier receiving a battlefield injury and getting to a field hospital:

- World War I: 15 hours
- World War II: 9 hours
- Korean War: 3 hours
- Vietnam War: 0.5 hour

The Risk of a U.S. Soldier Dying at War
(1860–1992)

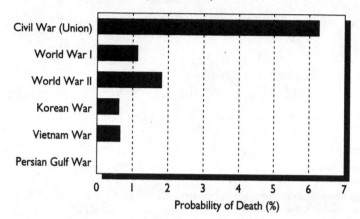

of internal political difficulties in various countries since 1945.

The proportion of those dying in wars during the 1980s who were civilians: 74%.

During the 1980s, on average there were 29,000,000 persons on active military duty worldwide; 40% of these forces belonged to NATO or Warsaw Pact countries.

The risks of command: During World War II, 1 general officer was killed for every 9,000 deaths in the lower ranks. In Vietnam, 1 general died for every 6,000 deaths in the lower ranks.

Is Saddam biding his time? The U.S. population will double in 99 years; Iraq's will double in 20 years.

The proportion of U.S. military fatalities in Operation Desert Storm due to "friendly fire": 11%.

8

Some Comparative Risks at a Glance

A SCALE OF RISKS

As I noted throughout this book, risks are typically presented in absolute terms (for example, "smoking is dangerous," "flying is safe," and so on). This lack of specificity makes it impossible to decide which are worth taking a chance on and which should be avoided altogether. The list on the following pages contains many of the risks discussed in this book; they are presented from most to least risky. A quick and easy way to figure out how risk-averse you are is to read down the list until you reach a risk that you feel reasonably comfortable running. Once you have found that, two good rules to follow are these:

1. To the extent that you have control over it, you should avoid all those activities mentioned in the list and elsewhere in this book that involve a greater level of risk than the one you are comfortable with.
2. You should *not* be phobic about engaging in activities with a smaller risk than that one.

Most of us tend to be comfortable with activities that carry annual risks of a more or less unpleasant nature smaller than 1 in 100,000 or 1 in 50,000. The slightly less risk-averse usually find that their habits and hobbies come with about a 1-in-10,000 chance of serious misfortune. If you find that you regularly engage in some high-risk activities while deliberately avoiding other, less risky ones, you might want to ask yourself whether that makes sense. It might, but it probably doesn't!

ANNUAL RISKS

If you are the "average American," the following are the risks you run *each year:*

You will be injured: 1 in 3.

Your baby will be born with a serious birth defect: 1 in 6.

You will have an auto accident: 1 in 12.

You will be injured if you play basketball regularly: 1 in 40.

You will have a heart attack (if you are over 35): 1 in 77.

You will be seriously injured at home: 1 in 81.

Your newborn baby will not survive until its first birthday: 1 in 100.

You will fracture your skull: 1 in 100.

You will die: 1 in 115.

Someone will attack you with a deadly weapon: 1 in 261.

You will die of heart disease: 1 in 340.

You will injure yourself on a chair or bed: 1 in 400.

You will die of cancer: 1 in 500.

You will attempt suicide: 1 in 600.

Someone in your household will die in an accident: 1 in 700.

You will have a fatal accident if you are a skydiver:
1 in 1,000.

You will get prostate cancer (if you're male) or breast cancer (if you're female): 1 in 1,000.

You will die from a stroke: 1 in 1,700.

You will die on the job if you are a coal miner or farmer:
1 in 2,300.

You will be raped (if you're a female): 1 in 2,500.

You will die in an accident: 1 in 2,900.

You will deliberately kill yourself (if you're male):
1 in 5,000.

You will die in an auto accident: 1 in 5,000.

You will die of breast cancer (if you're female): 1 in 5,000.

You will injure yourself shaving: 1 in 7,000.

You will be killed in the line of duty if you're a police officer: 1 in 7,700.

You will be murdered: 1 in 11,000.

You will die of AIDS: 1 in 11,000.

You will die in pregnancy or childbirth if you're an expectant mother: 1 in 14,000.

You will deliberately kill yourself (female): 1 in 20,000.

You will die from a fall: 1 in 20,000.

You will die in an accident at work: 1 in 26,000.

You will be killed by a car while walking: 1 in 40,000.

You will die in a fire: 1 in 50,000.

You will drown: 1 in 50,000.

You will be stabbed to death: 1 in 60,000.

If you are a nonsmoker married to a smoker, you will die of lung cancer from his smoking: 1 in 60,000.

You will die of complications from surgery: 1 in 80,000.

You will die from lung cancer caused by exposure to naturally occurring levels of radon gas: 1 in 83,000.

You will die from poisoning (excluding suicide): 1 in 86,000.

You (females) will die from toxic shock syndrome caused by the use of tampons: 1 in 100,000.

You will die riding your bicycle: 1 in 130,000.

You will choke to death on food: 1 in 160,000.

You will die in an airplane crash: 1 in 250,000.

An object will fall on you, killing you: 1 in 290,000.

You will be electrocuted: 1 in 350,000.

You will die in your bathtub: 1 in 1,000,000.

You will be killed by an animal: 1 in 2,000,000.

You will be killed by lightning: 1 in 2,000,000.

You will be killed in a tornado: 1 in 2,000,000.

You will die from falling out of bed: 1 in 2,000,000.

You will freeze to death: 1 in 3,000,000.

LIFETIME RISKS

The following list presents some of the *lifetime* risks that you, the average American, run over the course of your life:

You will die of heart disease: 1 in 3.

You will be the victim of a violent crime: 1 in 3.

You will die of cancer: 1 in 5.

You will be raped (if you're female): 1 in 11.

You will die of a stroke: 1 in 14.

You will go to prison (if you're male): 1 in 40.

You will die in an auto accident: 1 in 45.

You will deliberately kill yourself: 1 in 72.

You will be murdered: 1 in 93.

You will die of AIDS: 1 in 97.

You will die in an airplane crash: 1 in 4,000.

You will die in childbirth if you're a mother with three children: 1 in 5,000.

You will be killed by a dog: 1 in 700,000.

MEN (AND OCCASIONALLY WOMEN) AT RISK

It is widely known, of course, that men generally die four or five years younger than women do and there is a higher rate of infant mortality among boys than girls. It is less widely appreciated that between these extremes of infancy and old age, men consistently run a greater risk of dying than women.

Often, the difference is not merely a matter of a few percentage points; for many activities and diseases, men run a 200 percent to 2,000 percent greater chance of dying than women.

It is a staggering thought—especially for the men among us—that there is never an age, from birth through old age, when the male death rate is not substantially higher than the female death rate. Some examples may drive this point home. Of 1,000 babies born,

Males at first outnumber females by about 2 percent.

By the age of 25, their numbers are about equal.

By 35, women have a surplus of about 2 percent.

By 45, there are 4 percent more women than men.

By 55, women have an advantage of 7 percent.

By 65, there are 14 percent more women than men.

By 75 and over, there are 30 percent more women than men. Two-thirds of the women born 75 years ago are still alive, while fewer than 47 percent of the men are.

There are doubtless many reasons for this striking disparity. But one fact seems inescapable: Men, in both their professional and their private lives, are generally at much greater risk of injury or death than women. Why this should be remains a mystery. In some cases, the higher levels of risk are a result of life-style choices, gender roles, or occupation. But in other cases, the answer seems to lie in biology rather than preference or social role. The causes are thus a mix of nature and nurture, whatever their specific character. The figures on the next few pages do not explain this phenomenon, but they do make it vivid.

Males are *twice* as likely as females to die from the following causes:

Excessive cold

Motor vehicle accidents

Mouth cancers

Accidental poisoning

Sudden Infant Death Syndrome

Lung cancer

Emphysema

Liver disease and cirrhosis

Tuberculosis

Bladder cancer

Dog bites

Heart disease

And these perils claim the lives of *at least three times* as many males as females:

Accidents in general (3:1)

Homicide (3:1)

Poisonous animals or insects (3:1)

Suffocation (3:1)

Bicycle accidents (3:1)

Alcoholism (3:1)

Drug dependency (3:1)

Lightning (4:1)

Muscular dystrophy (4:1)

Accidental drowning (4:1)

Suicide (4:1)

Accidental stabbing (5:1)

Sports-related death (6:1)

Airplane crashes (6:1)

Falling from buildings (7:1)

Boating accidents (7:1)

Firearms accidents (7:1)

AIDS (8:1)

Fire (9:1)

Train accidents (9:1)

Explosive devices (9:1)

Falling into holes (10:1)

Falling from ladders (12:1)

Glider crashes (13:1)

Overexertion (15:1)

Accidental electrocution (16:1)

Machinery accidents (24:1)

Police gunfire (32:1)

War (60:1)

Prostate cancer (—)

Although the odds are clearly not very encouraging for the male of the species, the deck is not stacked against him completely. Women are at least twice as likely as men to die from the causes indicated below:

Skin diseases (2:1)

Urinary tract diseases (2:1)

Mental disorders (2:1)

Homicide by strangulation or hanging (2:1)

Diseases of the musculoskeletal system (3:1)

Senility (3:1)

Breast cancer (170:1)

Pregnancy and childbirth (—)

Uterine cancer (—)

RISK AND RACE

If sex is the most powerful predictor of risk level, race is a close second. In the United States, blacks live shorter lives, have higher levels of infant mortality, more frequently fall prey prematurely to disease, and run much greater risks of being murdered than do whites. This is particularly true for black males, whose greater risk exposure both as men and as blacks generates a life expectancy that is 8.5 years shorter than a black female's and 7.5 years shorter than a white male's.

Blacks are at least twice as likely as whites to die from the following:

Cerebrovascular diseases (2:1)

Fetal death (2:1)

Death in early infancy (2:1)

Sudden Infant Death Syndrome (2:1)

Septicemia (2:1)

Liver disease (2:1)

Diabetes (2:1)

Pneumonia (2:1)

Accidental poisoning (2:1)

Drowning (2:1)

AIDS (among men) (3:1)

Asthma (3:1)

Fire (3:1)

Nephritis (3:1)

Appendicitis (3:1)

Meningitis (3:1)

Tuberculosis (4:1)

Complications of pregnancy (4:1)

Excessive cold (among men) (5:1)

Hypertensive heart disease (5:1)

Being killed by a police officer (5:1)

Whooping cough (6:1)

Homicide (6:1)

Infant deaths from AIDS (8:1)

AIDS (among women) (9:1)

There are, however, a small number of perils that are at least twice as likely to be the death of whites as of blacks:

Suicide (2:1)

Mental disorders (among women) (2:1)

Falling (among women) (2:1)

Testicular cancer (among men) (3:1)

Coronary heart disease (3:1)

Water transport accidents (among men) (10:1)

Sources

Introduction

Office of Management and Budget.

C. Meltlin, "Milk Drinking, Other Beverage Habits and Lung Cancer Risk," *International Journal of Cancer* 43 (1989).

P. Holst et al., *British Medical Journal* 297 (1988).

Chapter 1

ACCIDENTAL DEATHS

National Safety Council.

National Center for Health Statistics.

S. Conn, et al., *What Counts* (New York: Holt, Rinehart, and Winston, 1991).

The Guardian Weekly, April 11, 1993.

J. Urquhart, et al., *Risk Watch* (New York: Facts on File, 1984).

The World Almanac (Mahwah, NJ: Funk & Wagnalls, 1992).

DEATH BY FIRE

National Safety Council.

M. Wilson, et al., *Saving Children* (Oxford: Oxford University Press, 1991).

National Center for Health Statistics.

S. Flexner, *The Pessimist's Guide to History* (New York: Avon Books, 1992).

The World Almanac (Mahwah, NJ: Funk & Wagnalls, 1992).

B. Cohen, "How to Assess the Risks You Face," *Consumer's Research* (June 1992).

R. Mourareau, *Fires in Buildings* (London: Elsevier, 1988).

S. Brobeck, et al., *The Product Safety Book* (New York: Dutton, 1983).

ACCIDENTAL INJURIES
National Safety Council.
S. Brobeck, et al., *The Product Safety Book* (New York: Dutton, 1983).
T. Heymann, *On an Average Day in the Soviet Union* (New York: Fawcett, 1990).

RISKS ON THE JOB
National Safety Council.
M. Benarde, *Our Precarious Habitat* (New York: John Wiley & Sons, Inc., 1989).
The Economist, March 20, 1993.
M. Cooper, ed., *Risk* (Oxford: Oxford University Press, 1985).
The World Almanac (Mahwah, NJ: Funk & Wagnalls, 1992).
B. Cohen, "How to Assess the Risks You Face," *Consumers' Research* (June 1992).
Health Effects Institute.
L. Krantz, *What the Odds Are* (New York: Harper and Row, 1992).
National Safe Workplace Institute.

A LITTLE ACCIDENT GEOGRAPHY
National Safety Council.

SPORTS ACCIDENTS
Journal of the American Medical Association.
National Safety Council.
Henry Solomon, *The Exercise Myth* (New York: Harcourt Brace Jovanovich, 1984).
M. Cooper, ed., *Risk* (Oxford: Oxford University Press, 1985).

Chapter 2

AUTO RISKS

National Safety Council.

U.S. Department of Transportation.

J. Wilson et al., *Crime and Human Nature* (New York: Simon & Schuster, 1985).

L. Evans et al., "Serious or Fatal Driver Injury Rate," *Accident Analysis and Prevention* 19 (1987).

National Center for Health Statistics.

Transportation Research Record, No. 1270.

S. Conn et al., *What Counts* (New York: Holt, Rinehart, and Winston, 1991).

Institution of Civil Engineers.

A. Hacker, *U/S.* (New York: Viking, 1983).

THE WHERE AND WHEN OF CAR ACCIDENTS

National Safety Council.

Texas Transportation Institute, Texas A&M University.

J. Urquhart et al., *Risk Watch* (New York: Facts on File, 1984).

SAFETY DEVICES

National Center for Health Statistics.

D. Viano, "Estimates of Fatal Chest and Abdominal Prevention in Side-Impact Crashes," *Journal of Safety Research* 20 (1989).

B. Cohen, "How to Assess the Risks You Face," *Consumer's Research* (June 1992).

The Economist, 4 December 1993.

Insurance Institute for Highway Safety.

M. Wilson et al., *Saving Children* (Oxford: Oxford University Press, 1991).

BIKES, MOTORBIKES, AND PEDESTRIANS
National Safety Council.
J. Urquhart et al., *Risk Watch* (New York: Facts on File, 1984).
M. Benarde, *Our Precarious Habitat* (New York: John Wiley & Sons, Inc., 1989).
H. Lewes, *Technological Risk* (New York: Norton, 1990).

AIR TRAVEL
C. Oster, Jr., et al., *Why Airplanes Crash: Aviation Safety in a Changing World* (Oxford: Oxford University Press, 1992).
National Safety Council.
L. Taylor, *Air Travel: How Safe Is It?* (Oxford: BSP Books, 1988).
T. Heymann, *On an Average Day* (New York: Fawcett, 1989).
C. Perrow, *Normal Accidents* (New York: Basic Books, 1984).
International Airline Passengers Association.
The National Times, December 1992.

BUSES, TRAINS, AND SHIPS
National Safety Council.
The World Almanac (Mahwah, NJ: Funk & Wagnalls, 1992).
CNN, 22 December 1992.
C. Perrow, *Normal Accidents* (New York: Basic Books, 1984).

Chapter 3

U.S. Department of Health and Human Services.

INFECTIONS AND EPIDEMICS
National Academy of Sciences.
U.S. Department of Health and Human Services.
J. Urquhart et al., *Risk Watch* (New York: Facts on File, 1984).
F. Braudel, *Structure of Everyday Life* (New York: Harper & Row, 1982).

M. Benarde, *Our Precarious Habitat* (New York: John Wiley & Sons, Inc., 1989).

S. Flexner, *The Pessimist's Guide to History* (New York: Avon Books, 1992).

J. Kandell, *La Capital* (New York: Henry Holt, 1988).

1992 Information Please Environmental Almanac (Boston: Houghton Mifflin, 1992).

CANCER AND HEART DISEASE

American Cancer Society.

U.S. Department of Health and Human Services.

S. Conn et al., *What Counts* (New York: Holt, Rinehart, and Winston, 1991).

M. Benarde, *Our Precarious Habitat* (New York: John Wiley & Sons, Inc., 1989).

National Center for Health Statistics.

R. Gabler, *Is Your Water Safe to Drink?* (Mount Vernon, NY: Consumer's Union, 1988).

Surgeon General's Report on Nutrition and Health 1990 (Washington, D.C.: U.S. Government Printing Office, 1990).

J. Urquhart et al., *Risk Watch* (New York: Facts on File, 1984).

GENERAL HEALTH AND DISEASE

S. Conn et al., *What Counts* (New York: Holt, Rinehart, and Winston, 1991).

C. Schoenfeld, *Retirement 901* (Madison: Magna, 1993).

The World Almanac (Mahwah, N.J.: Funk & Wagnalls, 1992).

The Guardian, 5 September 1993.

U.S. Centers for Disease Control.

National Academy of Sciences.

E. Gold, ed., *The Changing Risk of Disease in Women* (Lexington, MA: Heath, 1987).

National Center for Health Statistics.

The Economist, 4 December 1993.

National Center for Infectious Diseases.

U.S. Department of Commerce.

H. Roberts, ed., *Women's Health Counts* (London: Routledge, Chapman, and Hall, 1990).

CNN, 7 January 1993.

B. Goldman, *The Truth about Where You Live* (New York: Times Books, 1991).

Surgeon General's Report on Nutrition and Health 1990. (Washington, D.C.: U.S. Government Printing Office, 1990).

T. Heymann, *On an Average Day* (New York: Fawcett, 1989).

S. Brobeck et al., *The Product Safety Book* (New York: Dutton, 1983).

A. Pope et al., eds., *Disability in America* (Washington, D.C.: National Academy Press, 1991).

CONCEPTION, ABORTION, AND PREGNANCY

E. Gold, ed., *The Changing Risk of Disease in Women* (Lexington, MA: Heath, 1984).

National Center for Health Statistics.

J. Urquhart et al., *Risk Watch* (New York: Facts on File, 1984).

S. Conn et al., *What Counts* (New York: Holt, Rinehart, and Winston, 1991).

U.S. Department of Commerce.

EXERCISE AND HEALTH RISK

H. Solomon, *The Exercise Myth* (New York: Harcourt Brace Jovanovich, 1984).

The Economist, 20 December 1992.

MALPRACTICE

S. Conn et al., *What Counts* (New York: Holt, Rinehart, and Winston, 1991).

M. Cooper, ed., *Risk* (Oxford: Oxford University Press, 1985).

S. Flexner, *The Pessimist's Guide to History* (New York: Avon Books, 1992).
National Center for Health Statistics.

Chapter 4

D. Russell, *Rape in Marriage* (New York: Macmillan, 1982).

GENERAL CRIME RISKS
U.S. Department of Justice, Federal Bureau of Investigation.
National Council on Crime and Delinquency.
U.S. Department of Justice, Bureau of Justice Statistics.
National Education Association survey, reported in *The Nose,* January 1993.
Insurance Institute for Highway Safety.
C. Alexander, "Women as Victims of Crime," *The Changing Risk of Disease in Women,* ed. E. Gold (Lexington, MA: Heath & Co., 1984).
Information Please Almanac (Boston: Houghton Mifflin, 1993).
National Safe Workplace Institute.

TERRORISM
U.S. Department of Transportation, Federal Aviation Administration.
U.S. Department of State.
U.S. Department of Justice.
L. Taylor, *Air Travel: How Safe Is It?* (Oxford: BSP Books, 1988).

MURDER
U.S. Department of Health and Human Services.
U.S. Department of Justice.
L. Krantz, *What the Odds Are* (New York: Harper and Row, 1992).

K. Segrave, *Women Serial and Mass Murderers* (London: McFarland, 1992).

S. Flexner, *The Pessimist's Guide to History* (New York: Avon Books, 1992).

GENDER AND CRIME

U.S. Department of Justice, Federal Bureau of Investigation.

W. Farrell, *Why Men Are the Way They Are* (New York: Berkley, 1988).

C. Alexander, "Woman as Victims of Crime," in *The Changing Risk of Disease in Women,* ed. E. Gold (Lexington, MA: Heath, 1984).

J. Wilson et al., *Crime and Human Nature* (New York: Simon & Schuster, 1985).

U.S. Department of Justice, Bureau of Justice Statistics.

D. Chapell, ed., *Forcible Rape* (New York: Columbia University Press, 1977).

L. Ellis, *Theories of Rape* (Hemisphere, 1989).

National Council on Crime and Delinquency

ALL IN THE FAMILY

J. Thornton, "Family Violence Emerges from the Shadows," *U.S. News & World Report* (23 January 1984): 66.

R. Flowers, *Demographics and Criminality* (New York, Greenwood Press, 1989).

R. Gelles, "The Myth of Battered Husbands," *Ms.* (October 1979).

S. Steinmetz, *Victimology* 2 (1977–78).

M. Straus et al., *Behind Closed Doors: Violence in the American Family* (New York: Doubleday, 1980).

U.S. Department of Justice, Federal Bureau of Investigation.

THE CRIMINALS

J. Wilson et al., *Crime and Human Nature* (New York: Simon & Schuster, 1985).

U.S. Department of Justice, Bureau of Justice Statistics.

C. Conn et al., eds., *What Counts* (New York: Holt, Rinehart, and Winston, 1991).

U.S. Department of Justice, Federal Bureau of Investigation.

National Institute of Justice.

THE MEN (AND WOMEN) IN BLUE

U.S. Department of Justice, Bureau of Justice Statistics.

C. Conn et al., eds., *What Counts* (New York: Holt, Rinehart, and Winston, 1991).

THE CRIMINAL JUSTICE SYSTEM

U.S. Department of Justice.

U.S. Department of Justice, Federal Bureau of Investigation.

Chapter 5

SEXUALLY TRANSMITTED DISEASES

U.S. Department of Health and Human Services.

The World Almanac (Mahwah, NJ: Funk & Wagnalls, 1992).

National Center for Infectious Diseases.

National Center for Health Statistics.

U.S. Department of Commerce.

1992 Information Please Environmental Almanac (Boston: Houghton Mifflin, 1992).

L. Krantz, *What the Odds Are* (New York: Harper and Row, 1992).

New York City Mayor's Commission on the Future of Child Health.

J. Urquhart et al., *Risk Watch* (New York: Facts on File, 1984).

CONCEPTION AND CONTRACEPTION

J. Urquhart et al., *Risk Watch* (New York: Facts on File, 1984).

R. Hatcher, *Contraceptive Technology* (New York: John Wiley & Sons, Inc., 1976).

U.S. Department of Health and Human Services.

A. Hacker, *U/S* (New York: Viking, 1983).

E. Gold, ed., *The Changing Risk of Disease in Women* (Lexington, MA: Heath, 1987).

G. Kunan, *New Book of World Rankings* (New York: Facts on File, 1991).

S. Brobeck et al., *The Product Safety Book* (New York: Dutton, 1983).

National Center for Health Statistics.

ABORTION

The World Almanac (Mahwah, NJ: Funk & Wagnalls, 1992).

U.S. Department of Justice.

A. Hacker, *U/S* (New York: Viking, 1983).

1992 Information Please Environmental Almanac (Boston: Houghton Mifflin, 1992).

U.S. Department of Health and Human Services.

National Academy of Sciences.

G. Kunan, *New Book of World Rankings* (New York: Facts on File, 1991).

C. Taeuber, *Statistical Handbook on Women in America* (Phoenix: Oryx, 1991).

S. Conn et al., *What Counts* (New York: Holt, Rinehart, and Winston, 1991).

American College of Obstetricians and Gynecologists.

Studies in Family Planning, September 1969.

BOOZE AND ILLICIT DRUGS

Distilled Spirits Council of the U.S.

Report from a study underwritten by the R. W. Johnson Foundation, 1993.

G. Kunan, *New Book of World Rankings* (New York: Facts on File, 1991).

J. Urquhart et al., *Risk Watch* (New York: Facts on File, 1984).

National Center for Health Statistics.

U.S. Department of Health and Human Services, Health Services and Mental Health Administration.

S. Brobeck et al., *The Product Safety Book* (New York: Dutton, 1983).

E. Gold, *The Changing Risk of Disease in Women* (Lexington, MA: Heath, 1984).

1992 Information Please Environmental Almanac (Boston: Houghton Mifflin, 1992).

National Safety Council.

American Journal of Cardiology 55 (1975).

B. Cohen, "How to Assess the Risks You Face," *Consumer's Research* (June 1992).

National Institute on Drug Abuse.

S. Conn et al., *What Counts* (New York: Holt, Rinehart, and Winston, 1991).

Scientific American (July 1993).

SMOKING

J. Urquhart et al., *Risk Watch* (New York: Facts on File, 1984).

1992 Information Please Environmental Almanac (Boston: Houghton Mifflin, 1992).

B. Cohen, "How to Assess the Risks You Face," *Consumers' Research* (June 1992).

National Health Interview Survey, 1990.

L. Krantz, *What the Odds Are* (New York: Harper and Row, 1992).

CNN News, 2 December 1992.

U.S. Department of Health and Human Services.

The Economist, 4 December 1993.

G. Kunan, *New Book of World Rankings* (New York: Facts on File, 1991).

EATING

Surgeon General's Report on Nutrition and Health 1990,
(Washington, D.C.: U.S. Government Printing Office,
1990).

B. Cohen, "How to Assess the Risks You Face," *Consumers'*
Research (June 1992).

E. Gold, ed., *The Changing Risk of Disease in Women* (Lexington,
MA: Heath, 1987).

U.S. Department of Health and Human Services.

1992 Information Please Environmental Almanac (Boston: Houghton
Mifflin, 1992).

Chapter 6

NATURE DOING NASTY THINGS TO US

L. Krantz, *What the Odds Are* (New York: Harper and Row,
1992).

L. Taylor, *Air Travel: How Safe Is It?* (Oxford: BSP Books, 1988).

National Safety Council.

S. Conn et al., *What Counts* (New York: Holt, Rinehart, and
Winston, 1991).

T. Heymann, *On an Average Day* (New York: Fawcett, 1989).

National Center for Health Statistics.

National Earthquake Prediction Evaluation Council.

The World Almanac (Mahwah, NJ: Funk and Wagnalls, 1992).

S. Flexner, *The Pessimist's Guide to History* (New York: Avon
Books, 1992).

J. Eagleman et al., *Thunderstorms, Tornadoes and Building Damage*
(Lexington, MA: Heath, 1975).

R. Kates, "Natural Disasters and Development," *Wingspread*
Conference Background Paper (Racine, WI, October 19–22,
1975).

H. Lewes, *Technological Risk* (New York: Norton, 1990).

I. Holford, *Guinness Book of Weather Facts and Feats* (Enfield:
Guiness, 1985).

F. van der Leeden et al., *The Water Encyclopedia* (Chelsea, MI: Lewis, 1990).

J. Wright, ed., *Social Science and Natural Hazards* (Cambridge: Abt Books, 1981).

1992 Information Please Environmental Almanac (Boston: Houghton Mifflin, 1992).

N. Calder, *The Weather Machine* (New York: Viking, 1974).

M. Cooper, ed., *Risk* (Oxford: Oxford University Press, 1985).

R. Gabler, *Is Your Water Safe to Drink?* (Mount Vernon, NY: Consumers' Union, 1988).

B. Cohen, "How to Assess the Risks You Face," *Consumers' Research* (June 1992).

B. Goldman, *The Truth about Where You Live* (New York: Times Books, 1991).

R. Morris, *The End of the World* (New York: Anchor, 1980).

ARTIFICIAL RISKS AND DISASTERS

C. Perrow, *Normal Accidents* (New York: Basic Books, 1984).

W. Baldewicz, "Dam Failures," in R. Waller et al., *Low Probability / High Consequence Risk Analysis* (New York: Pleman Press, 1984).

The Economist, 21 November 1992.

The Sunday Times (London), 20 June 1993.

S. Conn et al., *What Counts* (New York: Holt, Rinehart, and Winston, 1991).

H. Lewes, *Technological Risk* (New York: Norton, 1990).

B. Cohen, "How to Assess the Risks You Face," *Consumers' Research* (June 1992).

B. Cohen, "Catalog of Risks Extended and Updated," *Health Physics* 61 (1991).

D. Elsom, *Atmospheric Pollution* (New York: Blackwell, 1987).

S. Flexner, *The Pessimist's Guide to History* (New York: Avon Books, 1992).

Harper's Index, December 1992.

R. Gabler, *Is Your Water Safe to Drink?* (Mount Vernon, NY: Consumers' Union, 1988).

Health Effects Institute.

National Wildlife Magazine, February–March 1992.

FDA Consumer 7 (1973).

1992 Information Please Environmental Almanac (Boston: Houghton Mifflin, 1992).

National Research Council.

I. Asimov, *A Choice of Catastrophes* (New York: Fawcett, 1989).

Chapter 7

THE GRIM REAPER

U.S. Department of Health and Human Services.

S. Conn et al., *What Counts* (New York: Holt, Rinehart, and Winston, 1991).

The World Almanac (Mahwah, NJ: Funk and Wagnalls, 1992).

C. Taeuber, *Statistical Handbook on Women in America* (Phoenix: Oryx, 1991).

M. Benarde, *Our Precarious Habitat* (New York: John Wiley & Sons, Inc., 1989).

U.S. Department of Commerce.

E. Gold, ed., *The Changing Risk of Disease in Women* (Lexington, MA: Heath, 1987).

National Center for Health Statistics.

1992 Information Please Environmental Almanac (Boston: Houghton Mifflin, 1992).

1990 International Union for Conservation of Nature and Natural Resources Red List of Threatened Animals.

CHILDREN AT RISK

T. Heymann, *On an Average Day* (New York: Fawcett, 1989).

National Safety Council.

INFANCY

New York City Mayor's Commission on the Future of Child Health.

National Committee for Adoption.

CNN, 16 January 1993.

The World Almanac (Mahwah, NJ: Funk and Wagnalls, 1992).

National Center for Health Statistics.

G. Kurian, *New Book of World Rankings* (New York: Facts on File, 1991).

1992 Information Please Environmental Almanac (Boston: Houghton Mifflin, 1992).

C. Taeuber, *Statistical Handbook on Women in America* (Phoenix: Oryx, 1991).

S. Conn et al., *What Counts* (New York: Holt, Rinehart, and Winston, 1991).

U.S. Department of Health and Human Services.

L. Krantz, *What the Odds Are* (New York: Harper and Row, 1992).

CHILDHOOD

M. Wilson et al., *Saving Children* (Oxford: Oxford University Press, 1991).

B. Goldman, *The Truth about Where You Live* (New York: Times Books, 1991).

S. Flexner, *The Pessimist's Guide to History* (New York: Avon Books, 1992).

M. Benarde, *Our Precarious Habitat* (New York: John Wiley & Sons, Inc., 1989).

R. Gots, *Toxic Risks* (Boca Raton: Lewis, 1993).

George Gallup, Jr., *The Gallup Report* (Princeton, NJ: 1982).

J. Garabino, "Incidence and Prevalence of Child Maltreatment," *Crime and Justice* 11 (1989).

American Humane Association.

D. Chappell et al., *Forcible Rape* (New York: Columbia University Press, 1977).

R. Gelles, *The Violent Home* (Beverly Hills: Sage, 1987).

J. McEvoy, "Middle-Class Violence," *Psychology Today* 4 (1970).

M. Straus et al., *Behind Closed Doors: Violence in the American Family* (New York: Doubleday, 1980).

SUICIDE

The World Almanac (Mahwah, NJ: Funk and Wagnalls, 1992).

U.S. Department of Health and Human Services.

National Center for Health Statistics.

L. Krantz, *What the Odds Are* (New York: Harper and Row, 1992).

B. Barraclough et al., *Suicide* (London: Croom Helm, 1987).

C. Leonard, *Understanding and Preventing Suicide* (Springfield, IL: Thomas, 1967).

U.S. Department of Commerce.

J. Urquhart et al., *Risk Watch* (New York: Facts on File, 1984).

J. Wilson et al., *Crime and Human Nature* (New York: Simon & Schuster, 1985).

S. Flexner, *The Pessimist's Guide to History* (New York: Avon Books, 1992).

M. Wilson et al., *Saving Children* (Oxford: Oxford University Press, 1991).

National Safety Council.

B. Cohen, "How to Assess the Risks You Face," *Consumers' Research* (June 1992).

WAR

S. Conn et al., *What Counts* (New York: Holt, Rinehart, and Winston, 1991).

1992 Information Please Environmental Almanac (Boston: Houghton Mifflin, 1992).

L. Krantz, *What the Odds Are* (New York: Harper and Row, 1992).

Harper's Magazine, February 1993.

J. Clarke et al., *Population and Disaster* (London: Blackwell, 1989).

R. Brown, *Fallen in Battle* (New York: Greenwood, 1988).

G. Kurian, *New Book of World Rankings* (New York: Facts on File, 1991).

U.S. Department of Defense.

S. Flexner, *The Pessimist's Guide to History* (New York: Avon Books, 1992).

M. Benarde, *Our Precarious Habitat* (New York: John Wiley & Sons, Inc., 1989).

Index of Risks

Index of Those at Risk

Author's Note

This book is not a work of science, nor a report of original research. It is, rather, a compendium of some of the things we have learned about risks is the last few decades. Clearly, a book like this is only as good as the numbers in it, and so I am indebted to literally thousands of anonymous epidemiologists, statisticians, actuaries, criminologists, designers of clinical trials, and others who work laboriously accumulating risk-related data. So far as possible, I have drawn on studies that are both timely and robust, but the various means by which experts make estimates of risk vary enormously from subject to subject. Even within the same subject, and even when risk investigators agree on the appropriate methods, different trials sometimes give quite divergent results. Moreover, the character of the risks themselves changes as we find new ways of curing disease, cleaning the environment, or fighting crime. Some of the statistics quoted here emerged from elaborately designed trials or extensive epidemiological analysis and are therefore probably highly reliable. Others simply present rough-and-ready extrapolations from observed relative frequencies and are thus more impressionistic than scientific. Moreover, almost all describe the levels of risk for that purely hypothetical creature, the average American. For such reasons, the figures here should be handled with a skepticism appropriate to the recognition that our understanding of many risks is still in a pretty primitive state.

Special thanks of a more personal sort go to Rachel and Heather for saving me from some serious mistakes.